At Home with André and Simone Weil

At Home with
André and Simone Weil

SYLVIE WEIL

Translated from the French by Benjamin Ivry

NORTHWESTERN UNIVERSITY PRESS

EVANSTON, ILLINOIS

Northwestern University Press
www.nupress.northwestern.edu

Printed in the United States of America

10   9   8   7   6   5   4   3   2   1

Library of Congress Cataloging-in-Publication Data

Weil, Sylvie.
    [Chez les Weil. English]
    At home with André and Simone Weil / Sylvie Weil ; translated from the French by Benjamin Ivry.
       p. cm.
    "Originally published as Chez les Weil: André et Simone, copyright © 2009 Buchet/Chastel, un département de Meta-Éditions."
    Includes bibliographical references.
    ISBN 978-0-8101-2704-3 (cloth : alk. paper)
    1. Weil, Sylvie—Family. 2. Authors, French—20th century—Biography. 3. Weil, Simone, 1909–1943. 4. Weil, André, 1906–1998. 5. Weil family. I. Ivry, Benjamin. II. Title.
PQ2683.E3463Z4613 2010
843.914—dc22

                                           2010014988

∞ The paper used in this publication meets the minimum requirements of the American National Standard for Information Sciences—Permanence of Paper for Printed Library Materials, ANSI Z39.48-1992.

For Eric

Contents

At Home with André and Simone Weil

Prologue

ON MORE THAN ONE OCCASION, I HAVE RENOUNCED SIMONE. I was ashamed of my affiliation with her, as if it were a defect. Some people may find that shocking, or simply foolish, but that's the way it is.

For example, my first lunch in Brooklyn with my new in-laws. I had already met the couple who are now my parents-in-law, but only now was I first meeting my sister-in-law, her husband, and two cousins who were curious to see the Frenchwoman whom their cousin Eric had unexpectedly wed two months earlier, in the shabby offices of the Bronx county clerk. Only three days ago cousin Eric, who always has to be different, finally deigned to phone his parents and tell them we are married. His mother hardly greeted the news with enthusiasm. She asked him how to spell my family name. Whew! At least my name is acceptable. But I am from Europe, a divorcee who already has a child. She hoped for someone better, grander, for her only son, and makes her feelings plain. She is unimpressed when Eric explains that my father, André Weil, is a "very great mathematician and indeed, one of the greatest."

"So?" she shoots back. "You were a brilliant mathematician too, until you decided to study medicine."

As soon as the food is served, my brother-in-law wastes no time in asking me:

"Weil? Might you be related to the philosopher, the one who became a Catholic?"

The ears of the two cousins perk up and they look at me with curiosity. One of them chimes in:

"She was also an anti-Semite. And, what's worse, during the War, when Jews were being slaughtered. We discussed her in one of my college courses. A disgrace."

The other cousin asks: "So you're related?"

Weakly, perfidiously, I reply:

"Ummm, no, well, maybe distantly related."

"Who are you talking about?" my father-in-law asks. His daughter informs him:

"Simone Weil. A French philosopher and a great mystic, or so they say. I have a Catholic colleague who admires her a lot."

But the cousin refuses to yield an inch.

"Of course Catholics admire her. She didn't want to be Jewish. She hated the Jews."

I look down at my plate, waiting for them to exhaust the subject, and then I give my new family a big smile. I resolve to sweep Simone under the carpet with a torrent of words:

"I may be related to Marcel Proust, his mother was a Weil, Jeanne Weil, in fact. There are many people named Weil. It's the most prevalent Alsatian Jewish name, which I believe dates back to the Napoleonic era when all the Levis changed their name to Weil. You know, until 1918, my family spelled the name 'Weill' with two *l*'s, which is the Alsatian spelling. But immediately after the First World War, a spelling error turned up in my grandfather's documents . . ."

I am safe. Simone is forgotten. In any case, my parents-in-law have never heard, nor are they curious, about her. Some years later, my sister-in-law will counterattack, after having seen a photo of my aunt on the cover of one of her books. She will say: "It's impossible that you are not related." But by then, it will no longer matter.

My mother-in-law will remain permanently convinced that her son is better in math than my father. Nothing will ever shake her from that creed. That's a mother for you.

Plato or Diophantus?

IN 1960S PARIS, A TWENTY-TWO-YEAR-OLD WHO HAS JUST
received a degree in classics rings the doorbell of one of the most
distinguished Sorbonne professors of Greek, whom she worships.
She hopes the professor will direct her thesis. The young graduate
adores Greek, and her composition teacher, a veteran of the Old
Guard who is not lavish with his compliments, has sworn that she
writes "like Demosthenes." She loves history and poetry.

She is not unduly impressed by the professor's splendid apartment overlooking the Luxembourg Gardens. Her own family has
one nearby, a more dilapidated version minus the gilding and ornament, and almost unfurnished, but whose smallest nook and
cranny is haunted by the ghost of a young dead woman, another
young graduate whom she herself resembles. Her only concern is
to carefully choose the words to explain to the professor, whom
she is visiting on that fine summer afternoon, how his lectures
have instilled in her the desire to become, in turn, why not, a
specialist in Greek.

The professor greets her in a friendly fashion, offering his hand,
and asks her to sit down before occupying a nearby armchair. He

looks at the graduate for a split second, and suddenly blurts out: "So, will it be Plato like your aunt or Diophantus like your dad?"

I do not remember the rest of the conversation, which doubtless was very brief. I must have stammered that I was neither a philosopher nor a mathematician. The great professor must have found me idiotic and tacitly pitied my illustrious relatives for the mediocrity of their descendant. As for myself, I was too young and intimidated, or perhaps too proud, to admit that his question paralyzed me, reducing me to insignificance. Petrified, I left hastily, and the heavy door of the magnificent home slammed shut on my ambitions to be a scholar of Greek. Did the great professor even notice the departure of the limp, amorphous, and invisible creature his words had created?

Sunshine in the Luxembourg's *jardin anglais* restored my body tissue to me, as well as a feeling of physical existence which was palpable and even pleasant. At least I would be left with that.

Phone Call

It is quite incorrect to believe that the dead are gone forever and never return to speak to the living. They return to speak to the living all the time; indeed, it is their main activity. For instance, my father telephones me fairly often. It always happens in the same way. I am seated at the dinner table, surrounded by several people, or else in a large drawing room during a reception. From a distance, I hear a telephone ringing. Someone answers, at times a family member and other times a stranger, perhaps a servant. Then the person appears and loudly calls that I am wanted on the telephone.

I immediately recognize the voice, needless to say. His way of pronouncing my name, placing the accent on the second syllable, a syllable which he stretches out like a rubber band which in turn is meant to draw me, pull me towards him. I reply, "Yes, André, yes it's me." I am somewhat shaken, I must admit. "Get me out of here, I'm bored," says my father, whom we always called André, I should say at once, since he did not want to be called Papa.

André never spoke quickly, not even in an emergency, and in

this case his plaintive tone, half-commanding and half-begging, simultaneously saddens and annoys me.

But he has already hung up. Before I had time to ask him if he could supply a few details about his situation, give me some news about my mother and grandparents, or tell me if he is enjoying, in spite of everything, his time spent with the one who, according to ancient Jewish tradition, was chosen as his study companion for eternity.

Still, I would have liked to know if this companion is Euler, as I had thought at the time of André's death. I felt that only Euler would be worthy to serve as fellow student for my father, the great mathematician, precisely in order to keep him from getting bored. Now André could once again do math; he was no longer too old, he was only dead. In the latter decades of his life, he had decided that instead of becoming depressed, like some of his old colleagues who strove to do math with less pliant brains, he would recycle himself. That was his own term for it. He recycled himself as a historian, producing his magisterial study on number theory throughout history, *Number Theory: An Approach Through History from Hammurapi to Legendre.** The frontispiece bears a photo of a bas-relief from the tomb of the Emperor Taizong of the Tang dynasty (seventh century), displaying a horse with a Chinese proverb written in calligraphy by the mathematician Shiing-Shen Chern: "The old horse knows the route."

The old horse had already worked and laughed quite enough with colleagues who had died before him. With these longtime friends he had founded, with youthful élan, passion, and a taste for student pranks, the celebrated group bearing the collective pseudonym of Bourbaki, after an imaginary mathematician named Nicolas Bourbaki, member of the Royal Academy of Poldavia, an equally imaginary Central European country. Now it was patently

*Translator's note: André Weil, *Number Theory: An Approach Through History from Hammurapi to Legendre* (Boston, Mass.: Birkhäuser, 1984).

clear that he needed something fresh, and I had total confidence in the powers of the beyond to reach the same conclusion as myself.

Only once did I manage to ask, before he could hang up:

"And how is Euler doing? Is he bored too? Are you bored together? In French, German, or Russian? Let me know."

My father, on the other end of the line, betrays his impatience not by speaking faster, but on the contrary, by hammering out his words in his unique way.

"So you'll never give up that loathsome craze for spending hours at a time glued to the telephone?"

After which, for a while he did not phone me, not even to call for help. I could only blame myself. I know him. I realize that he only picks up the phone when he has something specific and urgent to convey. Such as: "Get me out of here, I'm bored."

Of course, I would like to get him out of there, but he must understand that it is quite literally beyond my limited powers. For my part, I must remember that my progenitor is someone who gets bored easily, and therefore try not to blame myself unduly.

The Tunnel

My aunt is rather circumspect, and has only appeared to me twice. Over the years, I have inferred that she is extremely busy appearing to a bunch of other people who, from time to time, inform me of her apparitions.

Here is the story of her first intervention in my life. I was teaching at a small college in Vermont. The brisk air put a healthy color in my son's cheeks, and I played organ in the small Protestant church in the village where I lived. It was a church like the ones reproduced on postcards, with a neat slate roof and white-painted steeple. That year I was living a tragic, tender, and fairly vodka-soaked passion with a Russian dissident, a former "zek" who had done time in a Soviet gulag. I later learned that my fellow teachers were whispering behind my back that my masochistic fixation on this tormented Dostoyevskian character revealed all that I had in common with my aunt Simone.

One autumn, several of us on campus were afflicted with a kind of pneumonia which was then little understood. I was the only one to be hospitalized, the only one to spend several weeks in a delirium. I could no longer express myself in English, and a nurse from Quebec had to be located to tend me. I was the only one who was, for a brief time, considered a hopeless case.

I have rarely described this episode of my life, since although these phenomena are taken quite seriously in American spiritualist circles, which in no way appeal to me, the French intellectual milieu, to which I belong in spite of everything, rejects them entirely. Which would make it fairly bizarre to claim that during one feverish night, I saw my aunt—and what an aunt—appearing at the end of a long white tunnel.

Therefore even many years later, I am still quite sensitive to the ridiculousness of explaining that Simone Weil, yes, my aunt, appeared to me at the end of that famous white tunnel. It was a kind of funnel-shaped space, befogged but luminous, in which I saw her quite distinctly. At the very end, she was a dark silhouette enfolded in a cape, as she is in photos. She invited me to join her, using words which I do not retain exactly, but her reasoning was alluring. Yet she spoke to me without tenderness, as if it were a question of resolving a purely intellectual problem. I was seriously afraid that she might win out in this field where her superiority was assured, and I felt that I had to fight with all my strength. Still, I felt no hesitation, and later could still recall the argument which I made for not following her. Did I immediately launch my heavy artillery, against which she possessed no ammunition, namely my son, my eight-year-old whom I passionately loved and who needed me? I am not sure. Later I felt guilty for not having limited myself to this noble argument, instead having given lengthy explanations of how I loved the quiet pink skies during winter evenings, and the white birches against the glistening snow. How much I relished life. I think I even went so far as to frankly state that I loved my body and the pleasures which it procured for me. The niece of Simone Weil loved to make love, and was not ready to renounce it.

By the following day I was out of danger, but probably not because of the heroic resistance with which I faced down my illustrious aunt. Since I am already knee-deep in melodrama, there is nothing to be lost in going all the way. While I was arguing with Simone in a small Vermont hospital, a former boyfriend of mine who remained quite close despite the fact that he had been forced to cede his place to the gulag survivor (I always felt that the "spell" which Simone claimed to have cast on me as she fed me my baby bottle was that I would compensate, with my joie de vivre and somewhat amorous nature, for her own obstinate rejection of sexuality, what Simone Pétrement, in her admirably moving biography of my aunt, termed "gallantries") was walking up Broadway in New York City. He happened to meet a friend of his, a medical intern. The latter asked him why he looked so upset. It just so happened that two days before, one of his instructors had lectured about this recently identified type of pneumonia, as well as the antibiotic which cured most cases. My former boyfriend immediately rented a car and headed for Vermont, despite a threatening snowstorm. A good dime-store novel would detail how he was twice stopped for speeding, abandoned the rented car in a snowdrift, and hurled himself into the hospital like a snow-covered, befurred grizzly, after which he roused every doctor and nurse to be found. The novel would also describe how all the while, my present boyfriend, the zek who had become deeply religious during his years in the gulag, was arranging for my burial beside a charming Russian church perched high in the mountains. He had convinced the monks that Simone Weil's niece would not dishonor their tiny cemetery, and that while my soul was not strictly irreproachable, it would nevertheless not embarrass them.

The novel would also narrate the touching scene which occurred at my bedside. The extremely Christian Russian threw himself into the arms of the New York Jew and in his sonorous bass voice, sonorous even through the sobs, declared in a half-grandiose, half-despondent tone which only Russians can achieve: "She is dying. We both loved her."

It was sublime, but unfortunately the heroine of the tale was not sufficiently conscious to benefit from it.

My parents were traveling in China. By the time they learned the news of my ailment, I was already out of danger. My mother exclaimed with emotion that at the moment I fell ill, I was exactly the same age, give or take a couple of months, as my aunt when she died. My father just shrugged his shoulders.

As for myself, I could finally read Simone, since I was older than she was. I spent my long convalescence reading her *Notebooks* and last letters. In that tunnel where I refused to follow her, I felt as if I had jettisoned everything that was not essential. I had burned with fever, also burning away all but a simple propensity for life, the joy of watching the wind-blown snow fill my bedroom with milky light, and my merry little son, his shoelaces untied and coat misbuttoned, tottering home from school. I experienced joy just from breathing. In all modesty, I saw a parallel between my return to life, accompanied by a rejection of the sort of intellectual cynicism typical of young college professors, and certain sentences in which Simone mainly seemed to want to be touched. Spiritually or bodily? I felt that her famous desire for annihilation concealed something else.

I broke up with the *zek* who wanted to bury me.

It would be a shame not to mention that three years later, the intern whose brand-new knowledge of medicine had saved my life became my husband.

A Normal Little Girl

"Your aunt let herself starve to death, right?"

I am invited to tea at a classmate's home. I am twelve or thirteen years old. The question has just been asked me by my friend's grandmother, a fat, chirpy lady. Her eyes sparkle in my direction as she lifts a slice of fruit tart to her mouth and digs into it with her very long teeth.

Her daughter, my friend's mother, lays down the law:

"As for me, I admire her enormously. She saw things through to the end, a true ascetic."

"The parish priest talked about her, remember? He even mentioned the word 'saint.'"

"No, what he said was 'mystic.'"

"It's the same thing."

"No it isn't. But anyway, an ascetic, a real one."

Both turn to look at me again.

Busy chewing my cake while carefully not letting any crumbs fall, I am a normal little girl whom normal people can call upon to corroborate the admirable weirdness of her famous aunt. Admirable, yes, but also completely weird and abnormal, giving me a twofold satisfaction. I am normal, I am eating a slice of tart and also some flan, and all the while the blood of a quasi-saint, or so said the parish priest last week, flows in my veins. I win on two levels: while I benefit from a delicious teatime, I effortlessly share in my aunt's asceticism, and even sainthood, since my mere presence makes people think of her. I already know that ineluctably the words will follow:

"Honestly, it is remarkable how much you look like her."

I smile politely, giving a modest, serious smile, since the subject is not really amusing, but I am slightly ashamed of my hypocrisy. I feel guilty of betrayal, without knowing exactly whom I am betraying. I sense that I am a usurper, since those who fall into raptures over my resemblance to my aunt are unaware that my head is empty, that I never have even the tiniest thought which would be worthy of my aunt, who was so weird and so admirable. At twelve my dream instead would be to look like Gina Lollobrigida, so that Fanfan la Tulipe, played by Gérard Philipe, would fall in love with me. Three years later, I will envy the blonde ponytail and small, upturned nose of Brigitte Bardot.

The Saint's Tibia

SIMONE WAS THE YOUNG AUNT WHO DIED AT AGE THIRTY-FOUR, a few months after I was born, the one I looked like, the one I had to replace for her parents. She wrote to them eight days before dying: "You have another source of comfort," as part of a short letter penned in conscientious, childlike handwriting. The letter was preserved by my grandmother in an envelope which she inscribed: "Last letter from Simone, received after the telegram announcing her death." As a teenager, I knew which box contained this letter, and I reread it often. The source of comfort was me.

I grew up in Simone's shadow. Her myopic eyes, like my own, smiled at me through eyeglasses on photos which encircled my childhood and adolescence. Often I rediscovered her at unsuspected moments, in a bookstore window, on a book cover, sometimes even on posters. Her jet-black hair, like mine, abundant like mine, was wavy like mine.

How could I avoid defining myself in relation to her? Every day I was informed:

"You are prettier than your aunt but you are also a trifle thin, like her. Most important of all, don't let yourself get skinny, or you might become ugly, and wither and die young, as she did."

Inevitably they added: "It must be said that she took pleasure in uglifying herself."

I had no desire to die young, and even less to become ugly. I ate my bread and jam.

The first day of class each year, some teachers leaned over me to exclaim or whisper, according to their personalities:

"I admire your aunt so much."

Then they would add, in a dreamy manner:

"Luminous, luminous."

Their eyes shone, as proof that the teacher had retained a glimmer of that light, particles of which now bounced back upon me. What little girl would not be delighted to feel, if only for a moment, elevated above her classmates? Nevertheless, I was divided between an understandable pride and a shame at my own mediocrity. Of course, I was capable of winning scholastic awards, but I was well aware that the small glories of my ordinary schoolgirl's life had no share in the luminescence in question.

During some family lunches, it also happened that everyone suddenly looked at me as their forks froze in midair. I had made a gesture or facial expression which was typical of Simone.

Early on, I was asked if I had inherited my aunt's celebrated migraine headaches.

Described in this manner, my situation contains nothing extraordinary. Many people have grown up under the portrait or photo of a young uncle, an elder sister or brother, a father or mother who died too young, to whom they would be endlessly compared by their families for their entire lives. Almost always negatively, it goes without saying.

Being the son, daughter, nephew, or cousin of a famous person is already more unusual, but examples are abundant around us. Some families boast several members who succeed brilliantly in the same field, like the Pitoëffs in the world of theater, or the Fondas on-screen. The same phenomenon occurs in politics and science.

Yet how many people are fated to be the niece of a saint, to resemble her, and even bear her name, with the exception of a single syllable?

Acting or musical talent may be inherited from parents. An uncle's factory for making shoes, home appliances, or automobile tires may be inherited and, depending on ability, driven into riches or bankruptcy. One may follow in the footsteps of a father who is a doctor, lawyer, cobbler, or carpenter. Or a painter. And be as good as, or better than, he was, especially if he taught you his trade. Even if one is a lesser carpenter or dentist, it is possible to continue along the same lines.

It is impossible to carry on the business of a saint. This is a different sort of inheritance, which is, however, impossible to escape, unless one relocates to Patagonia or Lapland.

One day, an American intellectual who wrote a biography of my aunt, having herself grown up in the world of haute couture and high-class fashion magazines, told me very seriously that in order to escape an oppressive destiny, I should have chosen a career in the world which she herself had abandoned for university studies. Before meeting me, the same woman wrote to me, stating that a forthcoming encounter with me would be like a talisman for her.

A talisman. There it is. The word has been mentioned.

If you choose neither anonymity in a foreign world for which you have no taste, in this case that of fashion, nor Patagonian exile, there remains the interesting, albeit ambiguous, role of relic. The saint's tibia.

People whom you have never met in your life rush towards you, flushed with pleasure, saying "My God, what a resemblance. I recognized you right away."

Strange women (to all evidence, men are less subject to this kind of fetishism) ask you for permission to touch your hair which is "exactly like hers." At such times, it is good to recall that the vital and imperative role of the saint's tibia (whether from a male or female saint) is to be touched, rubbed, and kissed. Performing one's role conscientiously provides a certain kind of satisfaction. Complete strangers ask, point-blank and without the least embarrassment, about your religious beliefs. A subject which becomes all the more complicated when the saint whom you represent is a Jewish woman who spent her short life concocting reasons to be baptized, as well as other, equally imperative ones to do nothing of the kind. Who also found peculiar reasons to explain why you yourself should be baptized, a subject which will be discussed more fully below. In fact, still on the subject of baptism, sometimes one of these strangers grips your fingers in his and tells you how delighted he is to know that you have been baptized. When a priest does this, of course, he is entirely forgiven. Baptism is his stock-in-trade.

Someone you don't know, after chatting you up about one thing and another, in the intimate tones of an old friend, finally discloses that he is the cosmological twin of Simone Weil. He learned this from a reliable source and it has played a crucial part in his life. He appears to believe that this twinship grants him certain rights with you. He is so close to her, after all.

Strange men and women come up to you, extremely close, and admit that for long years they have experienced a passionate mystical relationship with your aunt, who has been dead for a half-century, and that they are deeply moved to be confronted today by your face, this face of a dead woman, this marvelous Weil face.

For a moment, you feel a little deceased yourself.

Being the tibia of a saint mandates a kind of social life which can be agreeable, since the people who come to rub against it, and therefore against you, are sometimes clever and congenial.

And yet, and yet. Being an adept, or true, tibia which is satisfied with its existence as a tibia requires enormous humility. A humility which my aunt, who aspired so ardently to be nothing, never bequeathed to me, and for good reason. Being nothing is absolutely not the same thing as being a tibia.

A tibia, even though it may be touched and have its hair pulled, is primarily an intermediary. A mouthpiece. When people

contemplate the tibia or caress it with a pious hand, they are looking for contact with the saint. They don't give a damn about the
tibia itself. Which is only normal.

A few years ago at a literary symposium in New York, I met an
American woman novelist, several of whose books I had enjoyed.
I was pleased to meet her. We spoke about literature and femi-
nism, of our individual writing projects, until a man whom I did
not know came over and whispered something in her ear. She let
out a shriek, hid her face in her hands for a second, and even emitted, I believe, a few tiny sobs. Then, her eyes riveted on me, she
breathlessly repeated, or rather hiccupped: "Her niece, her niece,
of course, I see now, oh my God, the actual niece of Simone Weil."
She no longer spoke to me, but studied me instead as one would
study a ghost. The unknown man who had informed her of my
identity remained anchored at her side, and nodded his head with
a gratified smile. As well he might. After some moments, weary of
this little scene and the role I was playing in it, I left them, only to
be joined at the buffet, in front of the salmon and asparagus with
mayonnaise, by a gentleman who, after introducing himself—he
was the novelist's husband—clasped me in his arms, saying: "You
cannot imagine the immense rapture and elation which this completely unexpected meeting has caused her. Believe me, she is still
overwrought, and will stay that way for a good while."

Living with Her

As a little girl, I thought they were doing their job. I had grandparents who worked all day long copying out one group of notebooks into another group of notebooks. They were not to be disturbed unduly. At noon they paused for half an hour to eat eggs cooked sunny-side up, a potato, and *fromage blanc*. It took slightly longer if they prepared lunch for us as well, my sister and myself.

After the war, not immediately afterward, but in 1948, the whole family finally returned to Paris to the apartment on the rue Auguste-Comte, across the street from the Luxembourg Gardens. We arrived first, followed by my grandparents. We drifted around the vast, empty, begrimed, and dilapidated apartment, one or two walls of which were scarred by bullets from the battle for the Liberation. But it still boasted unobstructed views of Paris, which the Germans had been forced to abandon when they ran off with the furniture. In the first postwar years, Doctor Louis Rapkine and his family drifted around it with us. In 1941, thanks to Rapkine, my parents had been able to leave France for the United States.

We slept on mattresses placed right on the floor, and sat on garden furniture brought back from Brazil. Still, there was a table, a solid, substantial wooden table positioned in the back bedroom, which had been Simone's room. As soon as they were back in Paris, my grandparents immediately sat down at either side of that table and opened the tall black notebooks which they had carried in their luggage from New York to Brazil, then to Switzerland and finally Paris, and began their job of copying.

I have in my possession several of these tall, black-covered notebooks purchased in New York where they were printed by the Dorothy Press on 125th Street, close to the apartment on Riverside Drive into which my aunt and her parents moved in 1942, where I would later live with my grandparents. These were genuine accounting ledgers with graph paper, taller than they were wide. Did my grandmother purchase them to keep accounts, when she earned a bit of money by sewing pearls onto ladies' hats and handbags, and embroidering baby clothes, like many other old lady refugees? Into these notebooks, as well as others in the French format, acquired later in Paris, my grandparents copied Simone's writings. Her New York notebooks were copied into the black notebooks. My grandfather took charge of copying texts with Greek passages, since he did it so impeccably.

I am done, broken, wrote Simone to a friend during the last weeks of her life, adding: *Perhaps the object might be provisionally re-assembled, but even this provisional reassembly can only be done by my parents.* And they would not be able, indeed would not be allowed, to do so, as the world conspired to prevent them from reaching their daughter and reassembling her. So instead they transcribed her. They kept her alive and continued to live with her. We lived with her, all of us. There was her room, with her photo on the wall, with her modest, tender, slightly sad smile and her eyes wide open behind her glasses, the "New York photo," the photo of Simone "just as we saw her for the last time," my grandmother would say. Beneath this photo was an old battered shipping trunk bearing the remnants of stickers with names of ships and addresses in New York and São Paulo. The trunk was covered with a doily, upon which stood a vase. Sometimes a visitor brought flowers, which were instantly placed in the vase on the old trunk, under the photo. Then there was the cupboard in which slumbered all those sentences, which she had written and which needed to be transcribed, the cupboard whose door I was so skilled at opening silently, in order to look for sentences about me.

My grandmother often spoke on the telephone. Her tinny voice, with its half-Belgian, half-Central European manner of stressing certain syllables, echoed throughout the apartment, since the telephone was situated in the hallway. For months on end she spoke about *Waiting for God*. My grandmother put the accent on the last word while her voice went down several notes, as if she were landing on the word "God." Were we waiting for God? Which God? My father only spoke to us about Greek and Hindu gods. At the neighborhood public school, where I attended elementary classes, the little girls spoke of Jesus, a God who was swallowed but must never be chewed, because then he would remain stuck in your mouth for your whole life. What God could my grandparents be waiting for, as they transcribed notebook after notebook?

I love reading Simone in these notebooks. Sentences and reflections which, I must admit, leave me indifferent or even repel me if I read them in print, move me deeply when I see them in my grandparents' handwriting, as I imagine the two of them seated facing one another at the wide wooden table which is now in my apartment, transcribing all day long, all week long, all month long. I see them, Bernard and Selma, whom everyone called Biri and Mime, leaning over their notebooks, eyeglasses perched on their noses, like two diligent elderly students. My grandmother's sharp profile, with her stiff gray bangs cut, without any coquetry, in a straight line across her forehead, and the softer profile of my grandfather, his still abundant moustache which scratched when he kissed you or put his ear to your stomach to examine you.

When I read the sentences transcribed by them, I feel that we are all still together, that I am sitting on their laps, and they are telling me about their dear daughter, whom I look like, and whose writings they read to me, just as when I was a child.

What did my grandparents think about when they transcribed, transcribed endlessly the many notebooks left behind by their daughter? From time to time, they exchanged a few fairly brief remarks, as people working on a project do. Biri spoke in a rather quiet voice, while Mime was louder. Sometimes she stopped transcribing in order to comment on the day's news, to express outrage over something they had read together in the newspaper the night before, or while eating lunch. "No, it's unbelievable, really, these people have lost all sense of shame." Her violently aspirated *h*'s, both familiar and foreign, were absurd, yet pleasingly so. In a spinning world, amidst ever-altering scenery, this aspirated *h* was like a fixed point, both heroic and laughable.

What did she think about during all those hours of transcribing my aunt's rounded, childlike handwriting, transposing this careful schoolgirl's writing into her own calligraphy, that of a nineteenth-century young lady of good upbringing? Sometimes she indulged in decorating words with majestic capital letters, while other times she remained more austere. It probably depended on her mood.

The pages transcribed by my grandfather, and he is the one who transcribes those strewn with problems, are scrupulously accurate. Did Simone write half a page, only to cross it all out? Bernard copies the same half page and crosses it out the same way. Nothing is left out, shortened, or diminished. Was there ever any question of doing so? Certainly not. After all, it is his daughter's! Boxed paragraphs, cross-outs, sentences crossed with a single curvy line, or many lines, and then repeated, everything is there, and each page corresponds exactly to the original. The Greek letters are wonderful. There is just one thing he is incapable of reproducing: the fact that Simone paid no attention to lines, and used unlined notebooks whenever possible. As an ex-officer, Bernard has a sense of discipline, a sense of the correct way of doing things, and he rigorously abides by the lines of the large black notebook. I cannot imagine him doing otherwise.

My grandmother behaves like her daughter. She too has always been a rebel. She shows a royal disdain for line divisions, and sometimes condenses three of Simone's pages into a single one of her own.

My grandfather's handwriting is less uniform than that of my grandmother, less ornate, but nonetheless meticulous, the writing of a doctor who wants his prescriptions to be legible and understandable.

What could he have been thinking of, he whose vocation was to heal and cure, when he transcribed so many sentences solely about finding joy in misery and privation, in denial of the body and worldly possessions? He who adored joking and handing out candy, whose letters to his two children were always filled with advice for their health and well-being, what did he think when he transcribed the following sentence written by his daughter: *I am not, and I consent not to be; because I am not the good, and I desire that only the good should be?** Philosophical talk, he doubtless told himself, something he never attempted to understand. And I am sure that in his heart of hearts, he also told himself that all of this was not worth one correct, well-formulated prescription. But his "poor little Simonette" went to the very end of things. And died of it. Did he ever have the feeling of a terrible defeat?

He who enjoyed slightly risqué jokes, medical jokes which made my grandmother scream in protest, whatever could he have thought when, rising to stretch his legs, he cast his eyes on the page upon which his wife had just transcribed in her elegant handwriting: *Sexuality. There is a mechanism in our bodies which, when it is triggered, makes us see good aspects in things down here. It must be allowed to rust until it is destroyed?*

And what did she think, she who had been madly in love with her husband, signing all her letters to him: *your little wife who hugs you tightly?*

---

*Translator's note: Simone Weil, *First and Last Notebooks*, trans. Richard Rees (Oxford: Oxford University Press, 1970), 102.

My grandmother jotted on the cover pages of the notebooks which Simone utilized in New York:

Written in New York.
She left America for London
on November 10, 1942.

And on the cover page of the black notebook, she similarly wrote:

Written in New York.
She left America
on November 10, 1942.

Like a poem on a gravestone.

As if she never failed to recall, on the original and copy both, that beastly autumn day when, on a Manhattan dock, she hugged her daughter for the last time, made sure for the last time that she was dressed warmly enough for the crossing, that she had not filled her valises with books alone, not just Plato's *Timaeus* and the *Bhagavad Gita*, but also winter sweaters and spare shoes.

Seated in their respective positions at the table, did my grandparents ever recall, almost involuntarily, a time when they still entertained illusions, only to immediately fall silent and start scratching away once again? That spring, 1941 in Marseilles when Mime, unseeing like all mothers, wrote to André who had just arrived in the United States: *In a package from Paris we received Simone's 'major work.' I shall type it and try to find someone who is leaving for New York to bring you a copy. It may interest someone at the New School and might open some kind of new prospect for Simone. If she could find a job, however modest, what joy and peace it would mean for us.*

Prospect, job, joy, peace . . . Did she truly believe it, even in 1941?

When Biri had transcribed a sufficient amount, he went out for a walk. Each time he returned, it was a little party. No sooner had the door closed, and his beret been tossed onto the coat hanger, than he would declare, in his mischievous teasing Alsatian way: "No *croquignoles* today, the baker was all sold out." My sister and I clamored, noisily leaping around him like puppies, sticking our hands into the pockets of his overcoat or raincoat, to find the tiny, crispy biscuits which we adored. And he, laughing at our enjoyment, would eat several of them with us.

Where to Find the Sugar Bowl

MY MOTHER ENDLESSLY REMINDS US, "YOU ARE THE DAUGHTERS of a genius." Often she adds that we are very fortunate.

Being a genius, my father obviously cannot remember where to find the sugar bowl, the silverware, or the coffeepot, nor even the words for each object in question. When he needs a knife or sugar, André makes a big hand gesture, a sort of windmill motion. Sometimes he moves both hands. Two windmills. It is up to us, my mother, sister, and myself, to decipher the windmills before running to look for the object.

When my sister and I complain (my mother never complains), he explains that since memory is not infinitely expandable, it should not be burdened with useless trivia. I do not know why the sugar bowl's location appears at the top of this list of useless trivia. From my father's little speech, we draw the conclusion that useless trivia may perfectly well burden our own lackluster brains, and that we can, without consequence, fill our heads with sugar bowls, coffeepots, place mats, cleansers, and dust-rags. Or else that we too must find a stratagem of escape. Obviously Simone had hit upon a stratagem, and never hindered her memory with need-

29

less details. Nor even, it must be said, with certain details which we found rather useful. One need only read the letters in which Mime states how she is going to do the housework and cooking for the young graduate, who had become a teacher. Not just do the housework, but also shopping, hanging up clothes, and making sure that the "*trollesse*" had enough underwear and handkerchiefs. All this time, with her memory unhindered, Simone would devote herself to all sorts of amusing activities, like ridiculing the lady principal of her lycée, or attending demonstrations with striking factory workers. Nevertheless, I observe that my grandmother was concerned and wondered if Simone was suitable for marriage. Or rather, feared that she was not. "Can you see her as the mother of a family?" she wrote to my grandfather.

Sometimes my sister and I dream of having a run-of-the-mill father. He would make coffee and toss salads. He would not prefer his work to us, and would tell us instead: "How pretty you look, my dear, tell me about what you did today." He would speak to us with words of affectionate banality.

Yes, but there is the problem. It would have been banal. Mediocre. We had been trained to despise everything which was not excellent. How disgusting to see the father of one of our classmates or friends on vacation playing cards or, even worse, sitting on the sofa watching television. We blush with shame for our unfortunate little friend. Our own father, shut up in his study, lines up numbers and symbols whose incomprehensible nature guarantees their excellence. He labors over a sum of fractions which the world's greatest mathematicians have been focused on for almost a century, unsuccessfully. One day—I must be around ten years old, since I am learning to add fractions—André writes for me on a thin strip of paper:

$$1 + \frac{1}{2^s} + \frac{1}{3^s} + \frac{1}{4^s} + \frac{1}{5^s} + \frac{1}{6^s} + \cdots$$

This surprises me:

"That's it? That's what you're working on?"

I slide the strip of paper into my arithmetic notebook and keep it there for a long time, like a magic formula.

When he is not busy doing math, he reads fat books covered with rough leather, on the pages of which can be seen very old, perfectly round holes dug out by medieval worms. Or else he passes through a museum while devoting himself to unbelievably profound notions about Van Gogh's paintings or Greek amphorae.

Daughter of a genius. Very early on, I learned not to disturb him when he was working, to maintain a devout silence when he listened to Bach cantatas on the radio Sunday mornings. During my whole childhood, I would discern the looks of terror in the eyes of his young colleagues. And as for me, it was a given that he would call me an idiot for not understanding my Latin assignment or an algebra problem. This could even, by dint of a small effort, be transformed into a source of pride. I accepted that he would go off traveling when I was sick, and that he would only listen to me distractedly, with his eyes trained on a book. I took pains to find potentially interesting conversational subjects for him, since nothing made him madder or more scornful than a conversation which he esteemed pointless. Whether during meals or outdoor walks. Pointless was his word for them. Yet what joy, when at dinnertime, between two mouthfuls, I managed to make a pertinent remark about *Athalie* or *Le Misanthrope*, or quote a few lines from *The Aeneid*. In this last case, it was necessary to brace yourself and recall that he did enjoy it, despite the inevitable, crushed and crushing "My poor girl, they are not even teaching you how to scan Latin verse properly."

For our genius of a father did not limit himself to math. His brain was an octopus, the tentacles of which extended in all directions. He could scan Latin verse and Greek verse as well, and it was as if we were hearing Homer or Theocritus in person. Not to mention the fact that he read Greek from volumes filled with characters which in no way resembled the ones in our Greek grammar or book of excerpts from Greek literature. He also read

Sanskrit, with its truly bizarre letters. He spoke Italian like Dante, Spanish like Cervantes, and so for almost every living language. And he rendered them less alive, it should be added.

Indeed, we were fortunate. At mealtimes, we could learn and learn . . .

Only here is the problem: there was a demon, a powerful and cunning demon, who, having selected us as an adoptive family, followed us on holiday, sat down at our dinner table, and, it might be said, never left us. This demon whispered to my sister and me that the only way to seize the right to forget, or better still, never even to have known where to find the sugar bowl and mops, was to recite Virgil throughout mealtimes. This solution was obviously impossible. So the demon, pitiless and logical, urged us to charge ahead in the opposite direction, and from the start of dinner, exchange all sorts of inanities which made us kids guffaw and annoyed my father. The reaction came quickly: "Oh, you're breaking my eardrums!" We knew what would come next: "I am removing your power of speech. In fact, I am cutting off your tongues and putting them in my pocket. You understand? Your two tongues are in my pocket and you cannot talk again until I give them back to you."

When we were little, we took him quite seriously. When we were a bit older, we played along with the game and shut up. We waited until he decided to give us back our tongues. André was more powerful and cunning than the demon.

Who Are We Congratulating Here?

D URING ALL MY YEARS IN LYCÉE, THEN AS A UNIVERSITY student, my father, who was at first a professor at the University of Chicago and later at the Institute for Advanced Study, in Princeton, wrote me long letters. I still have them. Their subject matter is rather diverse. Some are wholly devoted to the schedules of airlines or ocean liners, when vacation times drew near and I had to visit my parents in America. As a young man, my father had been an obsessive reader of railway timetables. For him, train times represented dreams, freedom, but also, at a certain period, meetings with my mother. He never really renounced this passion.

Most often, the paternal epistles discuss my studies, and fairly often in them, my father mentions his sister. Comparing us, to a certain extent. So, when I was a sixteen-year-old student at the Lycée Fénelon (a school which Simone had also attended), he wrote to me: *The doubts which you are feeling about your own intelligence make me think of my sister, who once wrote to someone, I don't remember who, in a letter which has been printed (and which people who write about her readily quote) that she seriously considered suicide, apparently around the age of fifteen or sixteen, "because of the mediocrity of her talents" (I think those are more or less the terms she uses). I must say that at the time, I myself never suspected that she was in such a state of mind. Be that as it may, you can see therefore that you are not the first person who, around this age, is visited by this kind of concern, even though it is rare that anyone considers suicide for that reason (my sister surely exaggerated matters a bit in retrospect). I need not tell you that it is equally wrong to believe either that academic success never has anything to do with intelligence, or that it is a precise indicator of intelligence. For an intelligent person to make good use of the intelligence which she has, it is highly useful for her to have a certain amount of self-confidence. Now, success (which at your age means academic success) helps a good deal in building self-confidence, which is what makes it advantageous.*

My first major academic success would occur soon thereafter, a first prize in the *concours général*.* The awards ceremony in the main amphitheater of the Sorbonne must have been rather grand. General de Gaulle personally presided over the event, surely in or-der to demonstrate that in France, the young people were magnifi-cent. I do not have the slightest recollection of the ceremony, apart from what General de Gaulle said to me, while shaking my hand.

Later that evening after the awards ceremony, I was, quite un-usually, in a café with a friend.

A newspaper vendor came in. "*France-Soir*, get your *France-Soir*, late edition." From a distance, my friend recognized the front-page photo. It should be added that it occupied the entire center of the page. My friend stuttered in astonishment as he bought a pa-per: "L-l-look, just l-l-look." It was me. At the precise moment when General de Gaulle, leaning towards me, shook my hand. Our intertwined hands were a blur, necessarily, since both were in motion. But our faces were in very clear focus. The general, his lips slightly protruding, so that the words which emerged were

---

*Translator's note: In France, the *concours général* is a nationwide test given annually to students of the *première* (eleventh grade) and *terminale* (twelfth and final grade) classes of lycées.

almost visible, was saying something friendly, while I, with eyes cast upward, watched him. With a modest, polite smile. Me and de Gaulle. Me, dressed in a pretty flowered dress which my mother had purchased at the Franck shop for the occasion, covered by my old white leather jacket, slightly soiled, which I kept on, perhaps shy of displaying my arms to this whole gathering. Or more likely having forgotten. At sixteen, does one think about one's jacket under such circumstances? Over the photo, in bold type, read the headline: "Daughter of the mathematician Maurice Weil (an annoying typo for my father)—winner of the *concours général*—receives her award from General de Gaulle personally."

One hour later, prominently displayed at a newsstand on the boulevard Saint-Michel, was the eighth and final edition, with the same large photo (while the other stories on the front page had changed) over which in the same bold type, the headline was now: "Niece of the philosopher Simone Weil, etc."

It had become a family affair.

All that evening, and all the next day, the telephone never stopped ringing. People made fun of my father, who "finally found a way to be mentioned on the front page of a newspaper, only to be—most unfortunately—conjured away by means of a mistaken first name." My mother's female friends telephoned to bewail that I had not taken off my old jacket. My mother did not wait to hear from them before abundantly wailing about it herself. The pretty dress from the Franck shop had been for nothing. For several weeks, the women of the family spoke about that unremoved jacket, to the exclusion of almost every other topic.

I had received a huge stack of books and an ample travel scholarship. And I had my photo on the front page of *France-Soir* with General de Gaulle, who leaned towards me, taking my hand in his. The photo showed that he was speaking. What did he say? He told me: "I admired your aunt very much." Not a word more, not even "Congratulations, Mademoiselle." Nothing. I remember it exactly. Not a word for me, the kid who had just achieved her first true academic success.

Moreover, I knew perfectly well that in London, he had asserted that my aunt, the same one, was completely mad. So much for admiring her.

Of course, I still keep those two issues of *France-Soir,* which I am looking at as I write these lines. I look cute, with my black hair smoothed down and parted in the middle, but really it is a shame I did not take off that jacket.

To Baptize Me or
Not to Baptize Me?

DURING SOME OF THE YEARS WHEN WE LIVED IN THE APARTMENT
on the rue Auguste-Comte, I would sleep on the sixth floor,
which was my grandparents' floor. On certain evenings, after I
was thought to be asleep, I would get up and silently open the
"manuscripts cupboard." I would remove the covers from boxes,
some made of cardboard, others of wood, into which were piled
notebooks and loose pages covered with the careful schoolgirl's
handwriting that I knew so well. My aunt's writings on philosophy
and history were as abstruse to me as the mathematical jottings
scattered on my father's work table. So I soon identified the boxes
containing notebooks and letters. In my nightgown, squatting or
sitting cross-legged directly on the floor, I would read: *Christ himself
descended and took me.* Only, I myself infused it with the turmoil
of budding sexuality. How praiseworthy and inscrutable was the
ghostly aunt who made up part of our daily landscape! While I
dreamed of Gérard Philipe, she got herself taken by Christ.

I quickly discovered that I was mentioned in almost all the last
letters to her parents and her brother. At thirteen, I had already
memorized many of the sentences about me. Some were very

pleasing, very flattering. *Sylvie with a sunny smile,* that was me. Others mystified me: *I have cast a spell on her and this will become apparent in a few years.* Of course, I asked myself if the famous spell which Simone had cast was already apparent. But what kind of spell was it?

Naturally, the letter from Simone which I reread most often was the amazing one in which she advises my father to have me baptized. In case of *more or less anti-Semitic legislation,* my aunt wrote, *it would probably be pleasant for her to enjoy certain advantages, without having committed any act of cowardice.* This sentence left me beside myself with anger. It seemed unworthy of my aunt, and of me. I spoke directly to Simone. So there was room in her head for this type of notion? So she had in her some deeply buried cowardice, which she unhesitatingly attributed to me? The same baptism which she refused for herself, she hurled at me, while herself remaining undefiled, either from baptism or its "advantages." She reserved the right to be a hero, while turning me into someone who would find it "probably pleasant" to enjoy the advantages accorded to baptized Jews. What sort of advantages? A theater box at the *Comédie-Française*? A well-paying job? A big apartment? What kind of contempt must she have had for the woman I was to become?

Nevertheless, the same letter pleased and amused me when Aunt Simone seemed to ponder my marriage at length, listing all my possible fiancés. This inventory dazzled me. I could see a parade in single file of the various fiancés she imagined for me, the Catholic fiancé, the Protestant one, the "son of observant Christians" (I saw my future parents-in-law going to Mass, spruced up in their Sunday best), the Jew, the Atheist, and the Buddhist. The last one intrigued me most of all, as I imagined him always wearing a scrumptiously exotic costume.

For a long time, my parents were reluctant to fulfill Simone's wish. My father wanted to get off lightly with a Protestant baptism. He tried to convince his sister accordingly. In vain. She responded that Protestant baptism is very *"canulant"* (a note for novices: this means "inconvenient" in the slang of students from the École Normale Supérieure). "*Canulant*" because Catholics do not recognize it, she writes. Then there reappeared the Catholic fiancé whom I could not marry as a result of the Protestant baptism. Even if, for his part, he did not mind—decidedly, Simone thought of everything—his parents might be upset, and they would disapprove of our marriage. Ultimately, it all would have been for nothing. Fortunately, the reverse was not true, and Catholic baptism should create no problem for a Protestant fiancé. I would keep all my options open. All in all, Aunt Simone was planning like a forward-thinking mother—a Jewish mother, in fact, even if the subject was baptism—who only sought the best for her child. I must have a baptism fit for anything and everything, which would open the greatest possible number of doors, produce advantages, and not cause me any trouble.

Finally I was baptized in a New York church, quite a while after my aunt's death, first to honor her memory, and then because my family had the idea, shared by many Jewish parents, that a certificate of baptism offers some kind of protection. It joined the documents which we stockpiled, alongside veterans' cards; diplomas; medals, if any; all sorts of identity papers; and visas. At the present time, I very much fear I have mislaid my certificate of baptism.

On the other hand, I still possess visas for Siam for the entire Weil family. I have Simone's passport right in front of me, stamped "Validated for travel to and stay in Bangkok; September 17, 1940; Marseilles." And the splendid seal of the Siamese consulate. That was another idea of Simone's. In Marseilles, my grandfather Biri waited in line all night to obtain these visas, which were extremely costly. Bangkok? How would they have traveled there?

I was told that on the day of my baptism, I had a lot of fun racing around, between the rows of chairs. I was much too young to understand that henceforth, a whole troop of wildly differing fiancés might aspire to marry me, totally unimpeded.

How did it all work out? Although I did not resort to "fanatical Judaism"—another quote from Simone's letter, but what could she have meant by it?—I did "return" to Judaism and married a Jewish man issuing from a strictly Orthodox environment. The only turn of events which she had not anticipated.

The Nuns

SOMETIMES I THINK ABOUT THE TWO LITTLE ITALIAN NUNS, no longer young but daintily petite in their stark white wimples and long dark cloaks, who came to discuss Simone with my father at the rue Auguste-Comte. This is more or less the message which they affably conveyed:

"Signor Weil, *la sua sorella* Simone Weil was a great intellectual and her reasonings are very fine, but we would have convinced her, Signor Weil, convinced and converted her, believe us. We would have baptized her for you."

They departed with a sprightly tread, pleased with their visit and proud of their certainty, while my father, wishing them a good trip back to Rome, respectfully held the elevator door open for them. Then, pensively, he told me with an amused little smile bereft of any irony:

"Perhaps it's a shame that Simone never met them."

Gefilte Fish

What if Saloméa, whom everyone called Selma, had adored her Alsatian mother-in-law instead of ridiculing her? What if each year she had brought Simone and André as well as her husband to the seder, the traditional Passover meal which Eugénie Weill prepared, instead of disdaining it? For she not only failed to bring the children, but persuaded her husband not to go either. What if she had encouraged her children to feel respect and affection for this grandmother with lovely white hair and prominent dark eyes, whose only wish was to worship them? Instead of transmitting the disgust which she herself felt for the old lady who sometimes stayed for several days at a time with them, bringing along, in fact, her kosher cooking pot and plates, and her Hebrew prayer book.

Had Selma forgotten, or was she trying to forget, that her own parents attended the Antwerp synagogue and observed Jewish holidays? I am rereading a letter dated September 24, 1895, from Félix, Selma's brother, to their father, Adolphe Grigorievitch Reinherz. Félix gently mocks his dear daddy for deciding to shorten his vacation in Ostende in order to attend Rosh Hashanah and Yom

Kippur services on Bouwmeesterstraat (literally "Master Builder Street," where the Great Synagogue, also called the Dutch Synagogue, was built two years earlier, in 1893). The twenty-year-old youth inquires: *Despite your radical opinions and your children's religious skepticism, do you insist on preserving our ancestors' sacred traditions?* The time spent at the synagogue will make his dear papa lose his nice holiday suntan, he asserts: *The Good Lord commands you to take advantage of the fine weather as much as possible and instructs you to take a walk on Mariakerke (a beach near Ostende) instead of on Bouwmeesterstraat.* He concludes: *Ooh la la! With these few goyish sentences, I fear I may spark my dear parents' anger and outrage, but I am relying on the liberalism of their ideas to forgive me for not following them in their religious path and daring to discuss the matter. In any event, I expect that you will not forbid me to work on that day, a ban which, I feel I ought to warn you, I will transgress without a single scruple.*

Thus did a current of rebellion waft among the Reinherz children.

What does this prove? Nothing, except that Simone Weil's biographers valiantly follow in the footsteps of Simone Pétrement, who, when mentioning Selma's parents, describes them as "progressive Jews who had never observed any religious practices," thereby deliberately expunging that facet of the Reinherz family. They are described as a cosmopolitan, cultured, and musical family. They were certainly all that, which did not prevent them from going to synagogue occasionally, or keeping their children at home during Jewish holidays. At least a collection of Hebrew poems written by Adolphe Grigorievitch is mentioned, a volume bound in red morocco, which my father described several times, bemoaning its disappearance. Were they *piyutim,* Jewish liturgical poems, or love poems, using imagery from the *Song of Songs?*

I might add that not once did it enter the minds of the "progressive" Jewish Reinherz family, nor the observant Weills, to marry a goy, a non-Jew, or dispense with a rabbi at weddings, any more than it did the rebellious, opera-loving Selma or the liberal-minded, atheistic doctor Bernard.

In several scholarly articles about my aunt, I have found that her violent rejection of everything Jewish is explained by her first contact as a very young girl with her paternal grandmother's oppressive form of Judaism, enough to terrify any sensitive child. I was stupefied to learn that my great-grandmother Eugénie had traumatized little Simone by her "stern" and "forbidding" piety. Yes, stupefaction, since after all, the commandments which Eugénie, an old woman, obeyed could hardly have been all that offensive. Certainly she washed her hands before meals. So did Doctor Weil and his family, and rather obsessively too.

Would Simone have been traumatized just because her grandmother did not take along her handbag or an umbrella when she went for a walk on Saturdays? Because she did not eat pork or shrimp?

It's simply absurd. My grandmother had been interviewed, and the words of a daughter-in-law who had always disliked her mother-in-law were taken at face value. I firmly believe that my grandmother retained a remnant of adolescent rebellion against her own parents as well.

As for myself, I had long heard a different description of sad, tenderhearted Eugénie, that lonely old lady who always felt like a foreigner in Paris, never mastering the French language, and whose favorite son, my grandfather, forsook her, or visited her alone, hastily and by chance, because of the hatred which his wife felt for her mother-in-law. This extremely mild grandparent only wanted to worship the little girl whom she called "Simoneleh," as well as the boy, of course, whom she sometimes called "Avromeleh," for André was named after her husband, the Alsatian grandfather, Abraham Weill.

Let us imagine for a moment. What if Selma had brought her children to eat matzoh and gefilte fish (a time-honored family recipe, for sure) cooked by their grandmother, if Simone had retained charming and tender memories of Pesach meals at the home of her "grandma Eugénie"? What if . . . ? Let us imagine, sure, why not?

The Beauty of Euclid

I READ IN ONE OF SIMONE'S NOTEBOOKS:

The axiomatic system of modern mathematicians. What are they seeking? They do mathematics without understanding its use.
(Ask André. Does he feel pleasure when he succeeds, or aesthetic joy?)

I read this question, followed by the parenthetical question, and suddenly, without altogether knowing why, I feel good. The parentheses, ordinary in themselves, harbor a small family reunion. And the family is mine. I could not care less about the axiomatic system of mathematicians, but I am experiencing a private pleasure, like overhearing my father's professional discussions, of which I understood nothing, but which nevertheless reassured me. Conversations in the odd language of mathematics structured the space inside which I breathed and dreamed, as much as the rustling patter of André's typewriter, or the walls and roof which shielded me from the rain.

Surely Simone remembered to ask her brother this question. Perhaps one day when they lunched together at their parents' home.

The Weil Quartet is seated at the vast kitchen table in the rue Auguste-Comte apartment, on the heavy Flemish furniture brought over from Antwerp. A pleasant warmth predominates, with the wide-open window overlooking the sun-drenched court-yard in which swallows, agitated by springtime, throw themselves into the void, then climb back towards the sky in noisy curlicues. Voices fill the high-ceilinged kitchen, those somewhat tinny, slow-paced Weil voices, strongly accentuated to the point of seeming to declaim Greek tragedy or German poetry, with aspirate *h*'s, especially in the case of Mime whom, irreverently mocking, I often delighted in imitating. Biri is listening attentively, nodding his head. I wonder what Mime is serving. Probably a choucroute. The Weil family loves choucroute. I prefer to think that on this day, Simone agrees to drink a glass of Alsatian wine with her brother. They are all in a good mood.

I sit with them; I pour myself a second glass of Riesling. Simone, leaning on her elbows at the table, her hands partly intertwined, in a pose which is typical of her, waits for the answer to her question.

What answer does André give his sister on this day? I believe that he tells her that mathematics is an art, not a science.

He speaks of the beauty to be found in mathematics, starting with the works of Euclid and Archimedes. He says that he always loved numbers and mathematical shapes because of their beauty.

Perhaps he stops there. All his life, André displayed extreme modesty in expressing his personal feelings. He would speak indirectly, quoting great writers. The day after my mother's death, he will ask me: "You know the page in Saint-Simon's *Memoirs* which the author divided with a sequence of his tears?" I answered: "Yes, André, I know." "Well, I am thinking about that page."

On the day of his lunch with Simone, he would have surely spoken to his sister about the famous text by Poincaré describing the state of exaltation which sparked the latter's discovery of Fuchsian functions.

Perhaps he already tells her what he will later write down, that "every mathematician worthy of the name has experienced, if only rarely, the state of lucid exaltation in which one thought succeeds another as if miraculously, and in which the unconscious (however one interprets this word) seems to play a role."*

He surely would have mentioned Gauss, who reportedly said,. "*Procreare jucundum*" (begetting is a pleasure), while adding: "*sed parturire molestum*" (but giving birth is a pain).

Does he also say to his virginal sister, as he would later say more than once, that the pleasure of experiencing thoughts following one another miraculously, and flowing from one another, is superior to sexual pleasure because it can last for several hours, indeed several days?

Why not? You can tell Simone anything, and sometimes she seems to think of herself as a man.

In terms of the "success" which his sister mentions, I can easily imagine André replying soberly, accentuating each word, just as he did when, as a student, I was wondering about my future and asked his opinion. He replied that he considered himself immeasurably lucky to have had a passion.

He did not experience only one passion! As a boy, he was passionate about croquet. During the summer of 1914, my grandmother wrote: *André is playing croquet from morning to night and, for the moment, nothing else interests him. How passionate this boy is! May he only be passionate about good things!* André was only eight years old. One month later he had developed *a real passion for geometry.*

"The best that you can hope for in this lowly world is to experience a passion, one which allows you to earn a living."

That is what my father told me.

---

*Translator's note: André Weil, *The Apprenticeship of a Mathematician*, trans. Jennifer Gage (Basel: Birkhäuser Verlag, 1992), 91.

A Genuine Relic?

THE SAINT'S TIBIA? OH, COME ON NOW! YOU MUST BE JOKING! Fine, I am quite aware that I am not a genuine tibia. Even if occasionally bunglers deal with me as if I were a tibia, I am not a genuine piece of saint's bone. Nor am I a bone fragment or a slice of veil, belt, or sandal. Certainly, she touched me, held me in her arms, and gave me my baby bottle. That should be the equivalent of a sandal touching a saint's foot. Yet in truth, it is nothing of the sort. I have pondered this tibia story and have concluded that I was wrong to write that "they don't give a damn about the tibia itself." People do give a damn about a genuine tibia, or even a sliver of genuine tibia. I want to set things straight.

Therefore I am subjected to some of the annoyances of being a relic, without enjoying any of the main advantages. As a genuine relic, people would not be content to cosset me for a few moments, touch my hair or emit quiet sobs of joy while looking at me, only to drop me like an old dishrag immediately afterward. A tibia is not an old dishrag, and must not be dropped, for fear it might splinter, or just get angry. Were I a genuine relic, I would enjoy enduring importance and visibility. A genuine tibia is something.

A false tibia is not. Or at least not over the long run. The proof is that after almost fainting from joy after learning that she spent a moment in the presence of Simone Weil's niece, the American novelist paid no further attention to me, except to shake my hand clingingly at the end of the evening. Whatever I might have had to say did not interest her in the least.

And that's where it hurts, since now and then I do feel like speaking. A relic does not talk. A relic has no inner life; it is a void, exclusively a relic, a conspectus, succedaneum, or substitute of the adored object, the true cross, the saint's body, the saint herself. I personally wanted my own existence. Which made me courageous in a certain way, but also a false relic.

A genuine relic never disappoints. It cures invalids, heals wounds, assures victory, and sometimes makes it rain. If today it does not grant the projected healing, victory, or miracle, we keep on pleading, and sometimes threatening, and hoping that sooner or later these will finally occur. But we do not abandon it. We nurture, cajole, protect, and shelter it in a sculpture or gem-encrusted reliquary, and no one would think of rudely turning his back on it.

While as for myself . . .

Necessarily, I am a disappointment. After the first instant of emotion in the presence of my myopic, bespectacled eyes, my mouth and hair which "are so similar to hers," the disappointment is major. I do not even know my aunt's works by heart. Therefore I cannot complete quotations which are held out to me like offerings, in the hopes of a real communion, an ablution, a total immersion. So many people have looked at me at this point with clear disappointment and saddened astonishment.

When some people find me diaphanous, I am not the one who is missing. They are the ones who do not see or hear me. They are the ones who dream of Simone when they see me, who throw her at me along with all her accoutrements, as a prelude to their remarks about me. The ones who inevitably add the word "also" in an accentuated manner, when they might speak to me of something I have done. As for me, even my modest demands make life difficult for them. It would be so nice if I could remain a tibia, if they could delight in communing with Simone Weil through me.

The genuine relic is a presence, whereas I am an absence from the viewpoint of the faithful (and sometimes even of the indifferent, since a form of contagiousness occurs). My identity is not being. Not being Simone.

When I am invited to participate in an interview, a panel, a conference, or to lecture on a subject having nothing to do with the fields which Simone explored—for example the novels which I wrote about the family of Rashi, the great eleventh-century Talmudic commentator, nothing to do with Simone, right, everyone agrees—nonetheless I am inevitably introduced as "Simone Weil, oh, sorry, pardon me, I meant to say . . ." Thus my contribution, or lecture, begins with what I am not. I am not my aunt. I have developed some potential reactions, according to the context and my mood. A slightly irritated pout, a lightly mocking little smile of the "I knew that would happen" variety, or an indulgent expression, as if to say "Anyone can make a mistake, and your error is utterly natural." Or else a charmingly broad smile, to say: "You shall see how much you will love me for myself."

My parents might have named me Françoise or Martine. Would that have changed anything? When I was a teenager, for a time I dreamed of being named Gwendolyn. An entirely different destiny would have been reserved for Gwendolyn Weil. She would not have become a tibia, a genuine or false one, she would have sailed round the world in a catamaran, or won fame in the perfume industry.

A few years ago, I wrote a play which was performed with some success and later published. During a luncheon in Paris, after a new staged reading of this play at the Théâtre de la Huchette, I enjoyed hearing compliments from one of the guests: "Theatrically excellent, and so moving, this play absolutely must be staged so that people can see it." Delighted, I reply in turn, but immediately notice the perplexed expression of the lady with whom I am speaking. I ask her if we are both talking about my play, and she replies: "Of course not. I meant Simone's *Venice Preserved*."

I am also accustomed to conversations which end abruptly.

For example, the phone rings. A male voice, quite ardent and friendly. The voice seeks to publish a text by my aunt. We are talking about the theater, I don't quite know why, possibly because the voice is actively involved in theater. I say, modestly smiling into the receiver, yet also with understandable hope, that I would like to send him my play, since it might interest him.

The voice, now extremely enthusiastically, even, shall I say, voraciously, says, "Aaaaaah? An unpublished play by Simone Weil?"

Me: "No. A published play by Sylvie Weil. Me."

The voice: "Ah."

More than abrupt. A draft of frigid air has slammed shut a door which thereafter separates the voice from me. The conversation ends swiftly, after I have granted permission to publish a page, a paragraph, or a sentence by my aunt. Hurried thanks and then, "Goodbye, Madame."

If the false tibia maintained a blog, it would invest thousands of compassionate computer screens with all the minor disillusionments of a diaphanous, indeed invisible thing. It would post online the lament of a decalcified tibia.

Of course, some people would respond sharply, as is the general rule with blogs, that it is diaphanous because it has little intrinsic value, and it should be delighted to be favored with the status of relic, whether genuine or false. This status accords it a certain undeniable importance, and it should not be a general pain in the ass with its whining and ridiculous fits of wounded pride.

They would doubtless be correct.

Even though . . .

Choo-Choo

"WHEN I WAS YOUNG, AT NIGHT WE WOULD HEAR THE LITTLE train from Les Halles marketplace. It made a comfortable sound, not loud enough to waken us, but if we were not already asleep, it was something pleasant and calming. It went 'choo-choo.'"

André says "choo-choo" in a falsetto voice, just as when he reads a Molière play to us and changes his vocal tone to represent the ingénue.

I would have loved André's Paris. I would have loved the nights interrupted by a gently rhythmic hissing. I would have said, "There it is, the train from the Halles is going by," and I would have gone back to sleep. I am surprised and moved that my father is divulging this kind of memory, that he enjoys recalling this sort of detail. I always imagine him absorbed in thoughts which are a thousand times too complex for me, or dreaming of distant splendors which I would find similarly out of reach. Yet tonight, it is the little train from Les Halles. And André, young and energetic, in shirtsleeves, his hair windswept, his back leaning against the balustrade of the seventh-floor balcony on the rue Auguste-Comte, against a background of the Panthéon dome. Behind his eyeglasses, his brown eyes are inquisitive. At least that is the impression which they often give, possibly because he is so nearsighted. A look which is insistent, not merely cast around, surely due to the fact that he has difficulty seeing.

Proud but nervous, I wonder what I can possibly say that might interest my father, while a long pink cloud like a roll of cotton candy unravels from the Panthéon up to the Saint-Jacques Tower, although the sky is already dark behind the Eiffel Tower. My sister is doing her homework on the table in the dining room, which is also the living room and my parents' bedroom. The Panthéon dome and buildings along the boulevard are reflected in the huge picture window, like a Mediterranean city, luminous, pink and white, so palpable that by contrast, the little girl leaning over her notebook seems but a reflection, and the table upon which she leans her elbows appears to be suspended in the air, at the level of rooftops, ready to vanish with the last rays of the sun.

Do You Want to Come with Me?

WHEN MY FATHER PHONES TO SAY THAT HE IS BORED, I WOULD so much like to suggest something diverting. If I knew where to reach him, I would phone back right away, without letting myself be discouraged by the fact that last time he hung up rather abruptly, and I would suggest taking a walk. Since I always walked with him. When I think about it, it feels as if we crisscrossed the whole world. Straddling the oceans, from one continent to the next, we traced wide curlicues into the planet along the route of his exile, which I would follow. At first, he walked briskly, and I had trouble keeping up. At first, he was so tall. By the end, naturally, he was much shorter, and we walked haltingly.

Still, there were many missed walks, about which I now feel a nagging regret. During my early teens, walking with André represented an intellectual program which on some days seemed beyond my powers. Or against which I was rebelling, anyway.

Now I would like to phone him back in order to propose one of those walks which I had refused. One Sunday morning, for instance, a Sunday in springtime when he is calling my name. Already donning his jacket, he lets fly: "It's been a long time since I walked along the quays. Do you want to come with me? We could go as far as the Louvre, where I'd like to look at some of the Titians again."

His "Do you want to come with me?" still resounds in my ears and makes me wistful, now that I am no longer the fourteen- or fifteen-year-old girl who, just when she is about to hurry over, yelling "Yes, I'm coming, wait for me!" is suddenly seized with anguish over what she can possibly talk about with him. Talking about myself is out of the question; I am not a subject for conversation. Nor can there be any question of speaking about my classmates, nor of the games which I play with my cousins in the forests of Châtenay-Malabry. I must find something uncommon and first-rate to tell him in order to prove my intelligence. What if he got bored with me?

In those days, I was seized by faintheartedness. An overpowering laziness enfeebled my tongue, and I would mutter: "No, another time, I have homework to do."

"Oh, okay!" He left by himself. I remained glued to my chair. I knew that shortly, my mother would come over and make me despair all the more by telling me: "You might have spoken to André about the novel which you are reading, surely that would have interested him." Those were the very words I myself was thinking, ever since the door closed behind my father. Again I started muttering about my Greek assignment and physics homework. She went away, but not before having signed off with a Parthian volley: "He was very disappointed."

Even as I was concocting a flurry of urgent tasks, I vowed to speak with him at lunchtime, to fill the void created by my indolence and restore that link which had been broken by my faintheartedness, through the use of words. One of my special anecdotes, with pithy, vivid, slightly ironic observations, just as he likes. I will make him laugh, for indeed he loves to laugh, and is never handsomer than when, throwing his head back, he lets out a great resonant laugh. He loves others to be amusing. I will amuse him.

Today, for sure, I will phone him and tell him: "Now then, I've seen something in the Luxembourg Gardens which you will like. The oh-so-dainty statue of Laure de Noves has been shrouded in leaves, and transformed into a forest creature. Her head is all that peeks out of a pyramid of dead leaves. It's very pretty."

He would join me and we would go to the Luxembourg Gardens.

We would walk briskly, our heads slightly bowed, with similar profiles, our eyeglasses perched on our noses.

It would be windy. Massive clouds, heavy with autumn rain, would glide away across the flat sky, from the Eiffel Tower to the Panthéon, only to depart even further, towards the Champagne region and our ancestral Alsace. Once again André would recount *The Cloud Messenger* by the Indian poet Kālidāsa, the tale of a cloud ordered to carry news from a young man to his beloved, from whom he is cruelly separated. I still look for, and sometimes even find, this cloud, "handsome as an elephant escorted by a flock of storks," in the sky on windy days.

We would mention other walks, other travels. He would ask me: "Do you have fond memories of our trip across America? I think you must have been twelve years old." I would tell him yes, and then begin to laugh.

Some memories are so enchanting and strange that we wonder if we have not dreamed them. One such is of André, the great and famous mathematician, the terrifying and arrogant André Weil, with a raincoat draped over his pajamas to shield him from a gentle rain, running across the courtyard of a shabby motel somewhere in the American West, in search of twenty-five cents.

Why was my father, dressed in his pajamas, desperately knocking on doors at the motel to beg for change? What had happened to him?

It so happened that in the ghastly room with two sagging, squeaking beds separated by a soiled curtain, his wife and his two daughters were watching a film on a TV that worked only when it was fed with quarters. André failed in his quest, no door opened to his knock, and we never learned the fate of the pretty young girl who dared not admit to her betrothed that she was gradually growing deaf and soon would not be able to hear the voice of her beloved without a cumbersome and unsexy hearing trumpet.

I would ask in turn: "Do you remember in Chicago, how the janitor predicted that you would succeed in life because every day he saw you at the window, seated at your office typewriter until after midnight?"

He would doubtless reply with the question: "Did I give the impression of working very hard?"

With a certain coquetry, he always took great care to produce the opposite impression, rather despising plodders and wonks.

I would say, "You never worked all the time. You went to museums and concerts. You took us sledding and taught us to skate on the frozen lake near the university."

If he accepts this first invitation, I have quite a stockpile of walks to suggest. They need only be disentangled and shaken lightly. Walks in Paris, Japan, and finally Princeton, near the Institute, where he was appointed in 1958 and remained for the rest of his life. These last walks are perhaps not the most delightful, but they are part of the stockpile, and there is no reason to despise them, or to let them be forgotten entirely. More delightful were the walks in Brazil, in the early years, and wintertime walks in Chicago. The walks in Chicago always have a backdrop of midwinter. Who knows why, but that's the way it is.

Sunday mornings, we walk up to the radio tower. In São Paulo, the radio tower is at the end of the world. It rises, a metal structure isolated on a hill, quite rudimentary and somewhat rusty, through which gusts of wind blow.

We take ample strides through the high grass. He is tall. I am short, and must be only four years old. I run and skip at his side, lifting my feet, clad in boots as protection against snakes. We are alone under the vast sky, and all I can see around me is grass, slanted by the gusts of wind. When I look up, the clouds are flying by at top speed.

When we reach the top, we delight in looking at the houses, so tiny and faraway down there, all the way down. Then we begin the downhill climb.

But here's André, raising both his arms in a drolly theatrical pose of despair, and shouting:

"Oh, woe is me! We are lost, we are lost, I have forgotten the way back home!"

I roar with laughter, shivering with joy. And if it were true? Nothing to fear, in any case, since I am with my father. He is tall and radiantly handsome in shirtsleeves, with his collar open and his dark hair swept by the wind. We are lost! There is nothing but the vast sky, darkening heavy clouds, grass through which wind is whistling. And us.

And here comes the rumble of thunder. At first from afar. Then a little nearer. I already know what André will say. Perhaps I even say it before he does:

"That was Zeus. He is not happy. Hera must have played another trick on him."

Of course, I know that Hera is Zeus's wife, who does nothing but play tricks on him.

"Give me your hand," orders my father.

We run as fast as ever we can. With my head thrown back, I let myself go, fast and faster until my feet are barely touching the ground, as the tall plants tickle my arms and thighs, as the gale whistles in my hair. I am about to take flight.

A bolt of lightning streaks across the now dark sky. Then another. Thunder resounds.

"You hear? Zeus is annoyed."

We hurtle down the slope, no longer lost, and will soon find the path to the house, on a tree-lined street, the gate to the yard, the *casinha*, the mimosa tree. A few more steps and plop, the raindrops splatter on my nose.

Opening the gate, crossing the yard, noting in passing the squadrons of fat, slimy greenish caterpillars sluggishly climbing the mimosa trunks, pausing only to pick a nasturtium, arriving at the porch. We are saved.

Zeus can wield his thunder all he likes, he will not get us.

Wide and lengthy avenues, along which sweeps a wind so violent as to take your breath away, a wind so cold that the tears which it causes freeze immediately on your cheeks. There is no question of pausing, or even slowing down, for then one might be transformed into an ice sculpture. Automobiles are shrouded with snow, great white swellings all along the sidewalks. Chicago.

My heavy boots are slowing me down but still I must run and run to keep up with my father, whose legs are so much longer than my own, and who pushes forward remarkably quickly, in his large dark overcoat, his head bowed and shoulders curved against the wind. His steps crack the thin layer of ice on the snow's surface. He wears bizarre headgear, of which he is somewhat proud, steel-gray in color with earflaps that fold down. He looks like a pilot from the golden age of aviation. With a runny nose, or rather with a tiny stalactite of ice at each nostril, he warns me:

"Watch out, cover your ears carefully. If they freeze, they will fall off onto the ground. If you hear a quiet snapping sound that goes 'snick,' like something falling on the ice, take a good look, because that might be one of your ears. It has to be picked up very quickly in order to be stuck back onto you. Of course, we can always give you a false one."

I slap my hands, enveloped in large mittens, onto my ears, over my woolen cap, but then my nose is at risk of falling off. Will I hear it fall off? Will I be able to find the poor little rosy ice-cube mislaid in the snow? Not very reassured, I hide my face behind my scarf.

We run up to the museum, where we are going to visit the black emaciated mummies, which sleep in their colorful sarcophagi, half-skinned carcasses with their bandages unraveled. Other times, we run up to the university, in order to study the photos of stars, as well as lunar and solar eclipses. My father climbs the stairs four steps at a time. Some students and young colleagues, warmly wrapped up in their parkas, greet him admiringly: "Hello, Professor!" They smile at me. I know several of them, who sometimes come to visit. I am the one who opens the door to them, and even though I am only eight or nine, I am asked if I don't mind going into "Professor's" office to show him my math homework. I am the barometer of the master's mood. They remain standing in the foyer which looks into my father's office. The moment he raises his voice, they slip away. Disappear. If everything goes well, and I am not called an idiot, then, after I come out, they go into the genius's den. I am proud of my role as scout.

My half-frozen toes hurt terribly, and still I must run, run not to fall behind André, who cannot possibly, I cannot imagine it, not even for a second, have benumbed feet and painful toes. My father is invincible.

A Two-Headed Genius

THE GENIUS HAD TWO HEADS. MY FATHER HAD A DOUBLE, a female double, a dead or ghostly double. For yes, in addition to being a saint, my aunt was a double of my father, whom she resembled like a twin. A pervasive double, as only a ghost may be who no longer has anything else to do. Who no longer teaches, nor is a militant, nor takes off to fight in Spain, nor has amazing encounters with Christ. And yet she is doing all that constantly, uninterruptedly, far more than living people manage to do.

A terrifying double for me, since I looked so much like her. I resembled the double of my father.

This female double spoke to me through my father's voice. Sometimes André would mimic Simone. It was effortless, so naturally did it come to him to make that little lopsided smile which I saw in photos of Simone. That ironic and proud smile which she wears in photos from Spain, for instance, where she is garbed in mechanic coveralls with the initials CNT (Confederación Nacional del Trabajo) stitched on the pocket. André also shared the somewhat slow, monotonous, but resolute way of talking so often mentioned by those who knew Simone.

"You know what my sister would have told you?" he asked. Without waiting for a response, he continued:

"She would have said . . ."

He raised his head proudly. His eyes shone behind his glasses. His sister's eyes must have shone in the same way, and emitted the same mischievous gleam.

" 'In Spain, I had more than one person shot for less than that!' That is what she would have said."

"But she never did shoot anyone!"

"No."

All the same, I was impressed. Simone could have had someone shot!

André loved quoting his sister. He would begin this way: "My sister had a habit of saying . . ."

It was almost always something ironic:

"For example, she would say: 'In your next life, you will be a housefly.' "

Everything which she had said seemed to be important.

André never described his sister as a woman. He said "my sister" in the same tone which he would have used to say "my brother." This tone is hard to define. He did not talk about her the way one talks about a woman. Besides, we were familiar with Simone's letters to her mother, which she signed "your son, Simon."

And this son Simon, my father's twin brother, was sacrosanct. One day, after reading certain pages of my aunt's notebooks, I told André that she seemed to have had moments of great sorrow. His response was scathing:

"What are you talking about? She was always very happy!"

Only once, when I was about fifteen, did I rebel. We were at the dinner table on the seventh floor of the rue Auguste-Comte. I no longer recall the subject of conversation. It is possible that, armed with my brand-new Voltairean beliefs, I declared in a peremptory tone that I could not understand how Simone wasted so much energy on hogwash. André's reply, that I was "speaking nonsense, whereas Simone . . ." must have irked me. I yelled at my father:

"Your sister was crazy! She saw visions!"

I was instantly appalled by what I had just said. But André had already left the table, without uttering a word.

My mother often told me that it was lucky for me that Simone was dead.

I believed her.

My aunt's biographers describe several occasions when Simone wept in the company of friends. For me, this came as a big surprise. This person whom my father always depicted as strong and derisive, could she cry? The double of my father, this macho double, really wept? I could not imagine it. I never really saw her as a female.

I felt that if ever the famous line "I am an irresistible force" applied to anyone since the days of Victor Hugo's *Hernani*, it was to André and Simone. Both were suffused with the sense of their mission on earth. For one, it was math and an immense appetite for life, while for the other, it was a far more complex plan which led her to a voluntary death. They always looked forward, without the least concern for those around them. Those around them, the family first and foremost, had to adapt to them.

In daily life, this awareness of their mission and what the world owed or did not owe them resulted in colossal arrogance. There is a Yiddish word which describes this degree of nerve. It is "chutzpah." Simone and André were two sides of the same coin. An identical chutzpah. The Weil chutzpah.

When a reckless man, or more often a reckless woman, would ask him what was the point of his work, he would haughtily and arrogantly retort: "Nothing! It has no point!"

Yet one day he admitted to a friend that he believed his sister had been greater than he: "I was only a mathematician."

Simone also pondered the uselessness of mathematics, and perhaps with a measure of contempt for mathematicians, she wrote: *The mathematician lives in a separate universe where objects are symbols. The relationship between the symbol and what it signifies declines; the interplay of exchanges among signs develops by and for itself.*

Which did not keep her from madly admiring her brother, and

even envying him for having access to a pure form of truth. She painstakingly acquired some knowledge of mathematics, covering page after page of her notebooks with calculations and diagrams. She also attended Bourbaki meetings, sitting alongside André. A photo shows the whole group seated on garden furniture, at Claude Chevalley's country home. They are young and high-spirited. André is waving a heavy bell over their heads. Simone is the only one leaning studiously over her notes.

Imbued with humility, Simone felt that the world owed her nothing, or rather owed her hardships and discomfort. Systematically refusing to accept a room with a bed, no matter where she was, she would demand to sleep on the ground, in the dining room or the kitchen. Her unfortunate hosts, who felt both helpless and guilty about this skinny girl sleeping on the ground like a dog, would try to discreetly slide some blankets under her sleeping bag. Their kitchen or dining room would soon be overrun with Simone's books, papers, and cigarettes.

It would have been so much more charitable of Simone to accept the room which had been prepared for her, without making any fuss. I often thought that my aunt must have been wildly charming for her friends to give in so readily to her most absurd and awkward demands. She has been described as having power over people. That is also a phrase which I recall hearing used to describe my father. Simone and André imposed themselves. They compelled respect.

André's demands were diametrically opposed to his sister's. Which turned out to be no more convenient for his hosts. Arriving at a friend's home, whether in the countryside or a foreign city, André, who totally lacked humility, felt that the world owed him the most comfortable room, and above all the one with the best view. He would not hide his annoyance if the only available room was dumpy, overlooking a courtyard or parking lot.

I have seen André successfully demand that museum galleries which were closed to the public be opened for him. I have seen

him, less illustriously, nearly trample old ladies at a theater in order to capture a front-row seat by force.

I recall one summer in Yugoslavia, when I was fourteen. We
traveled by boat all over the coast, making several stopovers. At
each port, only the first ones to embark would find places to sit
on the ship's bridge. My father had developed a highly effective
technique, which he called the "Charge of the Hoplite Array."* It
consisted of swinging around our luggage forcibly and mercilessly
to clear a path through the crowd.

During my teen years, there was naturally never any question
of imposing the "exemplary" and necessarily mythical "conduct"
of my late aunt as a standard to be imitated, as so often occurs
in families. The fact was that the lycée jests and minor rowdi-
ness which I sometimes concocted were merely pallid stunts compared to the "hoaxes" of "the *trollesse*," hoaxes which always filled
her mother and brother with admiration. I do not know how my
grandfather felt about them, as he rarely expressed himself on the
subject.

Therefore I could come home and recount with pride my
clashes with proctors and teachers. I was never reproached when I
repeatedly received an F in conduct, year after year. My father found
it only natural that I should be derisive and impudent. Too bad for
the teacher who was unable to win my respect. I was just following
in the tradition of the Weil chutzpah. Still, he warned me:

"Be careful, my daughter. If you go too far, these women will
make your life miserable. You must always gauge the risks."

Resembling the sister who was so strong and yet, according to
André, imprisoned by an omnipresent and overprotective mother,
had its advantages. One summer when my parents and I were va-
cationing in Brittany, it was planned that I would go visit an aunt
and some cousins in the region of the Creuse. To reach them, I
would have to change trains three times. Two weeks beforehand,

*Translator's note: The "Hoplite Array" refers to ancient Athenian infantry.

André wrote to each of the three stationmasters, explaining that his thirteen-year-old daughter was traveling alone, and asking them to look after me. All three responded that they would take care of me personally. Indeed, they were waiting for me. At each station as soon as the train stopped, I leapt onto the platform and, careful not to let anyone know I had arrived, I rushed by myself to my connecting train. When I told André about this after my return to Paris, he looked quite pleased.

"I did my fatherly duty and you did your daughterly duty."

No one ever accused André or Simone of hypocrisy, or even an excess of courtesy. Both disregarded the art of kindly words, the little compliments which make personal interactions so much easier. Both were incapable of displaying feelings which they did not experience. Once when an old farmer, the father of one of her friends, proudly recited an old-fashioned poem, Simone promptly told him it was asinine. She felt that this type of sincerity was part of her duty as a friend. Perhaps she inherited this view from her grandmother Hermine Reinherz, to whom Selma wrote as a young girl: *What a strange notion, to expect that we should be delighted with scoldings and flee compliments like the plague, as is your ideal.*

For André, this sincerity was not part of a program, but the results were identical.

One evening when my parents were attending a concert, there was a sudden disturbance in the nearby front row. The orchestra stopped playing; the paramedics arrived to tend to a man who had collapsed in his seat, placed him on a stretcher, and carried him away. A woman followed the stretcher-bearers up the aisle. The concert resumed. A few people exchanged whispers. André furiously ordered, "Quiet!" A lady turned around indignantly, saying: "Didn't you see? The gentleman died." André retorted: "So what? There are worse things than dying while listening to Mozart."

These words, unacceptably brutal according to the criteria of common politeness, in fact expressed one of André's deepest desires. That is, to die while listening to Mozart's music. He often expressed this wish, which, when the time came, could not be fulfilled, as I still regret deeply.

Nevertheless, I am consoled by André's voice, repeating what he must have told me a hundred times, starting when, as a little girl, I informed him of one of my childish sorrows:

"My poor girl, let that be a lesson to you. Haven't you understood yet that there is no justice in this world?"

Family Portrait

I HAVE FOUND A FAMILY PORTRAIT AMONG MY PAPERS. FOUR people are included in it. Eveline, Selma, Simone, and Bernard. My mother, grandmother, aunt, and grandfather. It is an unusual form of portraiture. There are no faces or smiles, no "look at the dresses they wore then" or "don't those two look alike!" Nothing like that. It is a penned family portrait. It is a small sheet of paper containing four sentences in four different handwritings.

Usually the person who does not appear in a photo is the one who took it. In this case, no one has taken anything, but someone receives. The person who does not appear is André. André is the one who would receive the page. But between the moment when the "photo" is "taken" and when André receives it, a fifth party has come to join the family group, in the form of a crude zigzag in dark blue pencil. Which makes me think this must be from early February 1940, when my father is imprisoned at Le Havre. Not having responded to conscription in September 1939, he was arrested in Helsinki, accused of being a Russian spy, sentenced to be executed, but shunted off, unexecuted, to Sweden, Denmark, England, and then finally back to France by the end of January

1940. He recounted these adventures in his *Apprenticeship of a Mathematician.*

The zigzag which unceremoniously slashes across the sentence representing my mother is the signature of the warden or prison director at Le Havre. It differs from the signatures decorating the letters my father would receive once he was transferred to the jail at Rouen.

Where did the Weil family sit for this fine portrait which I am now holding in my hands? Which landscape served as a backdrop, on a cold day during this first winter of the war?

At first, I imagined them seated around the kitchen table at the rue Auguste-Comte, while Mime served them something hot to cheer them. But after some thought, I decided that I was mistaken. From the kitchen of the rue AC, as we always called it, the four people in the family portrait would have taken time to write long letters to their beloved prisoner. This note was written hastily, at short notice.

The day after he arrived at the municipal prison of Le Havre, André sent a letter to his lawyer and his parents stating in terms just allusive enough to be understood by all, that if he were not allowed to work, he would contemplate suicide. The family was thrown into a panic. A friend, Doctor Louis Bercher, obtained leave to visit André in a medical capacity. He wrote to reassure the elder Weils that the upsetting letter was written to rattle the prison directors, who naturally went through all correspondence with a fine-toothed comb, and impel them to allow André to receive books, paper, and ink.

Because Bercher was admitted to see André, the Weil family instantly imagined that all visitors would be permitted, and the whole quartet, with Eveline replacing André for the occasion, hurried off to Le Havre. There they found themselves barred. No authorization, no visit.

Getting back to the family portrait. The most plausible scenario is that the four Weils go into a café, perhaps right across the street from the prison, to warm up while waiting for the next train back home. Surely one of the three women said: "At least we can send him a short message. They won't refuse to give him a short message."

Of course, Bernard agrees to write a short message, but is most anxious to abide by the rules.

I suspect that Selma was not the one to come up with this plan, despite her usual enterprising spirit. Instead, on that afternoon, I imagine her as being noisily resentful that she was sent away. That leaves Eveline and Simone. They both agree that it would be possible. Eveline is an optimist by nature, whereas Simone is always disposed to the zaniest ploys.

But in fact Selma may have made a scene, so strikingly heart-rending, lamenting in such a theatrical way (she was extraordinarily gifted at this kind of display, as I have witnessed repeatedly) that the gatekeeper told them: "All right, write to him and I will make sure he gets your letter, but hurry up because I go off duty in thirty minutes and the fellow who takes over will not be as helpful."

Simone always carried around paper or a pocket notebook. Yet the sheet in question is not torn from a notebook, nor did the page emerge from Simone's pocket, for then it would have been crumpled, stained from ink and tobacco. Whereas my "photo" is uncreased and pristine. They must have asked for a sheet of paper from the café owner.

Eveline, the young daughter-in-law who knows her rights, has already grabbed the paper and from her pretty handbag takes a blue-inked pen, a striking, almost turquoise blue. The pen is necessarily hers, since no Weil ever wrote in turquoise ink. As the wife, it is up to her to write first. And to expunge any remaining doubt, she begins by affirming her proprietary rights: **My André.** He belongs to her; no matter how the others may squawk, they must follow her in single file to approach the party who is absent, yet present in name, the essential purpose of this family gathering, this embryonic procession. She brandishes the banner which must be followed, a banner which reads "André," but an André described as "My," namely Eveline's. She flashes a subtle smile to the Weils who are waiting their turn, while drinking bad coffee. Her frightfully nice and polite smile proclaims: "Your genius belongs to me, your 'kid' with the glossy black hair, Simone's 'dear Noumenon' has become my Prince Charming, which doesn't thrill you, I know, but, let's face it, we love each other, and there is nothing you can do about it."

After her statement of ownership, she can allow herself to show a degree of generosity. She graciously resumes her place in the Weil tribe. She will express herself in the plural form. This is a group photo, a family portrait, she positions herself very close to them, snuggling up to them, playful, naughty, and heavily perfumed, since she knows they loathe perfume. It seems that perfumes give Bernard headaches and Selma asthma attacks. Eveline does not believe a word of it. She writes: ***All four of us are thinking of you and kiss you. Eveline.***

She passes the pen and paper to Selma, casting a glance at her with wide blue eyes framed by long, mascaraed eyelashes. She holds back a smile. She finds the Basque berets which her mother-in-law and sister-in-law are wearing to be frankly comical. I can hear her bright voice, much brighter than the Weil voices, saying: "Here, Mime, it's your turn."

Selma gazes with her close-set, piercing eyes at her elegant daughter-in-law. She says in a saccharine tone: "Fine, I thank you most kindly."

With an accent placed on the "kindly." I can hear it from here.

Selma takes the pen, realizes instantly that today her usual expressions of affection, her "my darling" and "my dear son," have no place on this page which she is sharing with a daughter-in-law whom she dislikes (the feeling is mutual). Little Eveline has annihilated them with her "My André." He belongs to her, and all the "my dear sons" in the world will not change the fact. And so Selma moves on directly to the heart of the matter, her son's health, a subject which by rights she possesses and worries over, as the she-wolf who once tended and nursed her little ones, and who, until her final breath, enjoyed describing the force with which

André sucked at the breast. **Bercher tells us that you are well, and we are delighted to hear it.** But before she passes the pen to Simone, she reaffirms her rights all the same, signing: **Your mother who loves you, S Weil.**

Tomorrow, she will write to André from Paris: *Eveline has been staying with us for the past few days, she looks healthy, and is as nice and brave as possible.* As if speaking about a twelve-year-old girl.

Simone must be holding her pen vertically, which makes her handwriting very small and pointy. She is the one who writes the most. She, the *"soror,"* as André sometimes calls her, the accomplice, the twin, she assumes the duty of reminding her brother that what matters most is his cerebral performance. She writes in a fine style. **I hope that you are composing poetry and preparing some . . .** (the word 'lovely' is crossed out. Had she wanted at first to mention lovely mathematics or lovely proofs?) **. . . fine theorems, and manage to keep from feeling that time passes too slowly.** She writes of poetry. As children, for hours on end, did they not play at *bouts-rimés?** No need to use paper. And then she uses the word "preparing," which implies: "You need only dream of theorems and stockpile them in your memory until you have paper, which will come soon, worry not, you know us, we will move heaven and earth."

She does not kiss him. They are not the sort of brother and sister who kiss. She concludes: **We think about you all the time. Simone.** If at first glance, she seems to go one step further than her sister-in-law's message, I am sure it is unwittingly, since I cannot imagine her for one moment indulging in this kind of competition. Quite simply, what she writes is the truth. In the coming weeks, she will repeatedly visit the courthouse to attend trials and observe how they are conducted, in order to be able to advise her brother later on. When Simone thinks about something, she thinks about it all the time. Never in her life has Eveline thought of anything all the time, not even of André, her great love, her

---

*Translator's note: *Bouts-rimés* is a game in which the players improvise rhymes.

Prince Charming, which is immensely advantageous for her own morale and the well-being of those around her.

Eveline does not look at what Simone is writing. I don't believe she is interested. The two sisters-in-law have a courteous relationship. Eveline, the pretty, blue-eyed woman, with whom the handsome and brilliant descendant of the Weil and Reinherz families is madly in love, looks down on Simone from the height of her dazzling femininity, her joie de vivre, and her petit bourgeois common sense. She finds Simone ridiculous, a madwoman, with her clothing worn inside-out and ink stains on the tip of her nose.

For her part, Simone gives a low rating for intelligence to this woman whom André brought home. She has a fairly macho attitude towards her. *My brother dominates her completely,* she will write to a correspondent. Doubtless, having seen life go on around her, and having read some novels, she is resigned to this notion, that a man, even a brilliant one, needs a woman. Her brother is a man, and Eveline, with her Guerlain perfume, her girlish, mischievous disposition, her lovely breasts, and her sensual nature, is the woman he needs.

All this will not prevent the two sisters-in-law from getting along wonderfully during the months of André's imprisonment. They will put up a common front. When he will be transferred to Rouen, and will be allowed visitors, they will often take the trip together, Eveline bearing shirts, socks, and soap, and Simone lugging books.

Finally, it is Bernard's turn to add a message. Bernard, the father of the family.

On a large and classic family photo taken at Mayenne in 1916, he is standing behind Selma, who sits solemnly wearing a huge hat, flanked by her two children. Bernard looks handsome, proud, and upright, in full-dress uniform. He served as a military doctor for the duration of the First World War.

Today, at the bottom of the page there is barely enough room left to write a sentence to his son. He carries his own pen and removes it from his pocket, or else borrows one from the café owner.

He uses black, not turquoise, ink for writing. He quickly jots: **We hope to have the pleasure of seeing you again soon, your father B Weil.**

Done.

This marvelously noncommittal sentence is, at first glance, endearing in its restraint and dignity. Yet just as I sometimes put a magnifying glass to a photo in order to better discern someone's features, I am focusing on this sentence and I also perceive anger and humiliation. The shame of an Alsatian who had been proud to serve under the French flag, and whose son is imprisoned for refusing to join his regiment when another war is declared.

Poor Bernard really has no luck at all. He does not have the children whom he deserves. He has a daughter who has just developed a project to parachute weapons and soldiers into Czechoslovakia, in order to organize the Czech anti-German resistance, and who has sworn that she will throw herself under a streetcar if she is not permitted to be among the first parachutists. He, the unfortunate father, does nothing but plead with all and sundry, from union organizers to senators, to protect his daughter, to tell her white lies if necessary, to keep her from risking her life excessively, in Spain, or Czechoslovakia, or who knows where. He seriously suspects that this is only the beginning.

And now his son is in the slammer for draft-dodging.

After giving their brief collective message to the prison gatekeeper, the four return to Paris.

Two days later, André is transferred to the military prison at Rouen. The family will be able to pour out their hearts in separate letters. Love letters exchanged with Eveline, in which there is much ado about flowers and music, and a profuse intellectual correspondence with Simone.

Selma writes about her impatience to see her son, her maternal affection, and mentions books which she will buy for him. She painstakingly includes her daughter-in-law in the family circle: *You can tell how impatiently all four of us are waiting for authorization to see you.*

74

Bernard writes on his prescription forms, which henceforth will only be used for family correspondence; he is elderly, and within six months, on October 3, 1940, anti-Semitic legislation will prevent him from practicing his profession. His tone becomes less curt. The retired officer has grown accustomed to his son's situation, and affection reasserts itself: *I cannot tell you how happy we are to know that your health is good. Would you allow me to offer you a bit of medical advice? Try to do a little exercise every day, if possible morning and night for ten to fifteen minutes at a time. I think you will still remember some calisthenics, otherwise I will try to draw a little diagram. We count the hours until the time when we can see you again. I embrace you affectionately. Your father, B. Weil.*

He takes the subject of fitness training deeply to heart. A few days later, he is on the attack again: *I believe that given your current lack of exercise, ten minutes of gymnastics every morning, if possible, will do you good. No doubt you will recall the calisthenics which we have done together so often.*

My mother often described the days which she and Simone spent together, when they went to visit André, the trip by train, the sandwich in a café. I would have given a lot to have seen Eveline and Simone, André's two women, together. The sight of them walking along the streets of Rouen must have been fairly striking. One wearing a shapeless skirt, men's shoes, and beret, while the other donned pretty hand-knit sweaters, a ravishing chapeau, and lipstick.

One evening in Paris, Simone, having apparently forgotten that they were supposed to have dinner together, arrived late to meet her at André's modest apartment on the ground floor of the rue Auguste-Comte. The two of them spent half the night seated on the floor with a jarful of cherries in brandy set between them. Simone started telling fairy tales, as was her custom. My mother listened with delight. She later told me repeatedly about this evening, a long night like a magical interlude in the middle of that winter during which the war broke out. But an incident surprised, puzzled, and impressed her. My mother was by nature physically affectionate. She could not resist the temptation to run her fingers through Simone's hair (it must have reminded her of André's, which she had not touched for several months), and while doing so, she exclaimed: "What magnificent hair you have, Simone."

As my mother told it: "Simone jerked away as if a snake had bitten her, and shouted 'Don't touch me!'"

This episode always interested me. Eveline believed that Simone was terrified of any caress. Was this, I asked myself, perhaps because she was dying to receive them? Did she feel defiled by this contact, by a caress from the pretty woman who slept with her brother?

Simone caught her breath, and continued with her story. Together they finished the jarful of cherries.

Sterling Ancestors:
From the Galician Side

In Jewish tradition, it is more or less required when writing about a renowned individual who is noted for exemplary morality, and especially one with a penchant for saintliness, to ascribe to the person a brilliant family tree, what in Hebrew is called *yichus*. An ancestry of rabbis and sages, Talmudic scholars of righteous piety combined with absolute humility. If possible, a lineage which goes all the way back to King David.

I have searched in vain among Simone's ancestors for men matching this description, or even for a single old rabbi who, like the great master Rabbi Yaakov ben Yakar of Worms, was said to have used his long white beard to sweep the floor before the Holy Ark.

Nonetheless, as a result of rummaging around our ancestry, by swimming against the current of several generations of respectable shopkeepers and presumably blameless businessmen, I managed to locate, in the small Galician city of Brody, one of Simone's great-great-grandfathers, who had masses of curly hair and a long beard, a Hebrew scholar who was so ungifted in money matters that his business went downhill. Without his forceful and brilliant wife, their six children might have starved. I was delighted by this information, and Grandfather Barasch (his first name has not survived), leaning over his books, and useless at business, is a sterling ancestor for Simone. My father often said that Jews could be divided into two categories: merchants or rabbis. Naturally, he classified himself, along with his sister, in the latter category, which did not keep him from taking pride in almost always selling what he called his "modest merchandise," or mathematical insight, at a respectable price.

But let us return to Grandfather Barasch. Born in Brody, after his wife died he moved to Lemberg to end his days in the house of his daughter Antonie. Which is how Hermine, André and Simone's grandmother, would spend her childhood in his company. Later, she would record her memories of him.

Personally, I am genuinely satisfied with this ancestor, seated at a table in Brody, sweeping the yellowed pages of an old Talmud with his ample beard, while his wife sold who knows what in the ground-floor shop of their two-story home, decorated with a wooden balcony.

I say the Talmud, but it was not necessarily the Talmud. He might have been reading the *Tanya*, or the *Collected Sayings* of Rabbi Shneur Zalman of Lyady, if he was attracted to Hasidism, since Galicia was one of the cradles of varied forms of exalted piety. I always believed that a certain number of globules directly originating from a Hasid of that region circulated in Aunt Simone's veins. On the other hand, he may have been reading books and pamphlets by the great reformers of the Haskalah, also known as the Enlightenment. The two movements, Hasidism and Haskalah, enjoyed equal importance among Galician Jews and fiercely competed, sometimes within a single family, during the mid-nineteenth century.

Later, in Lemberg, it would be amusing to imagine that Grandfather, with his now-white beard and curls, too absorbed in his reading to notice that curious little Hermine was watching him, was engrossed not in the Torah but Abraham Mapu's *Ahavat*

Ziyyon (*Love of Zion*), the first novel to be written in Hebrew. Mapu, who penned the bestseller, first published in Vilna in 1853, hoped to be the Eugène Sue or Alexandre Dumas of the Jews.

Without quite sharing that ambition, I have more than once considered writing a novel about Simone's maternal ancestors. The subject offered all the required elements for a nice fat novel of the sort which people like to read on winter nights in the countryside. Vast fields, forests, endless and ever-snowbound steppes, bandits, wolves, Cossacks, and pogroms.

Laziness, I think, prevented me. So much area to cover, in imagination, if not in reality. So many small cities to be described: Lemberg, Brody, Tarnopol, and Brzeżany. Plus the big ones: Vienna, Odessa, and Rostov-on-Don. The endless train travel, for Jews traveled a lot, despite the tolls which were levied upon them when they entered cities. They would move house, depending on the power of what my great-grandmother Hermine gingerly termed the "nasty little breeze of anti-Semitism."

So I decided to write a few chapter headings at least, not for a novel, but the actual and true family history which explains how fate led the Reinherz family to Paris, where in 1905 Selma would marry Bernard Weil, and where in 1906 André would be born, followed three years later by Simone.

Chapter the First. In which we see how, around 1810, the leader of a gang of bandits already notorious around Brody went into the shop of the blonde, lovely Mrs. Barasch whose husband was upstairs, airing his beard out over a volume of the Talmud. In another version of the story, it was a work of mystic piety or reformist pamphlet. The aforementioned Hebrew novel had not yet appeared.

What was the intention of the cruel bandit, much feared throughout the region? He came to tell Mrs. Barasch that he had heard that she was so religious, good, and charitable that she would never have anything to fear from him or his gang, and she could even leave the shop doors wide open, because anyone who harmed her would have to answer to him.

Chapter the Second. In which, still around 1810, another great-grandfather of Selma Weil, née Reinherz, was devoured by wolves in the region of Tarnopol.

An ancestor of Simone being devoured by wolves is a nice detail, I feel. The family is from Galicia, after all, and a little local color is not uncalled for. The truth, however, is less melodramatic. The ancestor, named Reinherz, was on a business trip, sleeping at an inn next to an open window. A rabid wolf came in through the window (recall that this occurred in the middle of endless forests and steppes), bit him in several places, and then escaped. The unfortunate traveler recovered from the bites but succumbed to rabies, leaving a grief-stricken, but resourceful, widow and an only son about whom we will hear more below.

Chapter the Third. How cholera, which raged in Moscow in 1848, would influence the destiny of the whole family, including the coming generations, since without cholera, André and Simone Weil would never have been born.

Here is why. Antonie was the youngest daughter of the bearded Hebrew scholar who was bad at business. She was a cute little blonde. When she reached marriageable age, her older sister Charlotte, who had already been married several years, in Odessa, to Simha (called Semion) Pinsker, a noted scholar of Near and Far Eastern studies, decided to marry off her beloved little sister to the son whom Simha (called Semion) had fathered during a first marriage. Cute Antonie was brought to Odessa where she spent a whole year at the Pinsker home, waiting for her fiancé, Lev, called Leon. This Leon Semyonovich Pinsker had just finished medical studies in Moscow. He was getting ready to return to Odessa when a cholera epidemic struck. Young Dr. Pinsker distinguished himself with heroic service at a Moscow hospital, but obviously had no time to return to his father's home in order to marry Antonie Barasch. Much later, after the pogroms of 1871 and 1881, Leon Pinsker would become the first theoretician of the Zionist movement, preceding Theodor Herzl.

One of Antonie's older brothers, deciding that Antonie had

waited long enough, arrived to bring her back home to Brody. On the way back, they passed through Lemberg, where they happened to meet Salomon Sternberg, the oldest son of a certain Zvi, called Hersch (both names mean "deer" or "antelope"), who kept a shop at Brzeżany. Salomon and Antonie liked each other right away, married at Brody, and set up house in Lemberg, where Hermine, named in honor of her grandfather Hersch, would be born in 1850. Whew!

Salomon Sternberg, a foreign exchange dealer and pawnbroker, was as bad at business as his father-in-law, old Barasch. He was obsessed with music, and spent most of his time playing Beethoven sonatas. More good genes for Simone and André.

Chapter the Fourth. How, during the same summer of 1848, Grigori Reinherz (the son of the man who was devoured by wolves) left his home town of Brody at the precise moment when a young rabbi who had been living there for only a few years was killed, poisoned by members of his own flock who felt he was too progressive and disposed to Reform ideas about Jewish worship.

The case of the poisoned rabbi is entirely factual, but nothing indicates that my ancestor was involved in this dreadful crime. Family history only records that this decent man was obliged to travel to Odessa to earn his living.

I pause here for a moment to state that the person whom I have just called Grigori surely did not have this Russian, and dreadfully Christian, first name when he left Brody. To be sure, his son, Simone's grandfather, possessed authorized papers and documents in the name of Adolphe Grigorievitch Reinherz. Which would have been normal in Russia. Still, I assume that the first name of Reinherz from Brody was Gershon, soon Russified by his partners and customers into Grisha, which is a diminutive for Grigori.

Since I'm on the subject of names, or more precisely Jewish names, in the family it was said that the earliest member of the Reinherz line (the one the wolf got, or maybe his father), when the Jews of the Austro-Hungarian Empire were given family names, must have generously bribed a civil servant to be gifted with the high-class name of Pure-Heart. Löwenherz, Lion-Heart, would not have been bad either, we thought. Meanwhile, we also imagined some poor guy lining up behind or in front of our ancestor, only to return home later with the much cheaper, but also less gracious, name of Gallstone.

But let us return to Gershon, called Grigori, whose son Adolphe will marry Hermine Sternberg. What follows is excerpted from Hermine's memoir, written around 1920 in Paris, in a modest little student notebook:

My father-in-law married quite young, and had a great deal of trouble supporting his large family, his five children, his mother, and his sister-in-law.

My mother-in-law was the epitome of charity. Her children even complained that her heart went out to the poor and dispossessed more than to them. When she had a little money, she gave it away almost to the point of lacking for her own family, and when it was all gone, she would donate any possessions without forethought.

Being very religious, she always went to synagogue on Saturdays and Jewish holidays. One year, her husband was astonished when on the Day of Atonement, she said she was too tired to go. When she was questioned further, she admitted having pawned her genuine pearl headband to help a relative in distress, and she did not want to appear in temple without this ornament.

My father-in-law, realizing that in Brody he could not earn enough to support his family as well as his wife's costly generosity, moved to Odessa, a wealthy city where he had many relatives. He brought with him his oldest son Adolphe, then aged eighteen.

This same young Adolphe would grow up to be the grandfather of André and Simone. The latter would be named Simone-Adolphine in his honor.

No one ever knew what the religious Mrs. Grigori Reinherz thought of the reforms advanced by the unfortunate rabbi who was so shamefully murdered.

Chapter the Fifth. How in the spring of 1857, Salomon Sternberg left Lemberg with his whole family, to move to Vienna, because he wanted his three children to learn to play Beethoven better than he did, an accomplishment which he decided, no doubt correctly, would be impossible to achieve in the Lemberg ghetto.

He was fortunate enough to be able to set up house in Vienna, having been preceded by a Sternberg uncle who had obtained the *Ehrenbürgerrecht,* or honorary citizenship. This was an extraordinary favor at a time when Jews were forbidden to stay in Vienna for more than five consecutive days.

The idealistic Salomon, besotted by classical music, did not strike it rich in Vienna, but his three children, Hermine, Henri, and Anna, did become outstanding pianists.

Chapter the Sixth. In which, to round out immediately the interesting description of Mrs. Grigori Reinherz, the author takes the liberty of leaping forward by two decades, arriving at a modest scene which occurred in September 1876.

In this early autumn, Adolphe Grigorievitch and Hermine Solomonovna Reinherz, who had married six years before, left Vienna, where they were visiting Hermine's parents, to return home to Rostov-on-Don.

Once again, Hermine will be allowed to express herself in her own words:

The trip was long and uncomfortable. First we stopped off at Brody. My parents-in-law were also staying there at the time, so we all stayed at the home of one of my mother-in-law's brothers.

I inspected this impoverished city, and the houses in which my mother and husband were born, which seemed dreary and dilapidated.

One day, standing next to my mother-in-law, I saw through the window the crowd of shabby-looking Jews swarming over the town square on the occasion of the High Holy Days. I asked her how she had managed to live in this place for so very long.

She replied that she would still love to live there, and in reaction to my astonishment, she added earnestly: "There are so many poor people here."

Does not this religious and charitable lady display some

charming chromosomes of sainthood, which will be transmitted to her great-granddaughter Simone? Minus the pearl headband, of course.

Chapter the Seventh. In which we return to the year 1870, and we perceive that the status of dowerless daughter (it will be recalled how poor Salomon was hopeless in business matters) was lucky for Hermine.

I could not expect any dowry from my parents, writes Hermine, *and I resolved not to accept the one which our wealthy relatives granted to impoverished family brides*.

Then came Adolphe Grigorievitch Reinherz, a man in his forties whose businesses (exporting grain and wool) had succeeded in Rostov, to the point where he could choose a dowerless bride. He fell in love with the attractive Hermine Sternberg, and married her. The latter had just turned twenty years old. The marriage was celebrated in Vienna on September 4, 1870. Right in the middle of the wedding dinner, someone entered to announce Napoleon III's surrender at Sedan, and the proclamation of the Republic in France.

Chapter the Eighth. In which poor Salomon, distressed about his beloved daughter going away to live in the land of the Cossacks, begged her tearfully at the last minute, when the train was already leaving the station, not to neglect her piano, that lifelong friend to whom he had introduced her, nor above all her Beethoven.

Also in which the Cossacks attack the train carrying the two newlyweds towards their future, and make off with Hermine's trousseau. But they neglect (or perhaps a big-hearted Cossack pitied the twenty-year-old bride) to snatch away her engagement ring.

Might it be mere family tales and legends that the train was besieged by Cossacks? Perhaps we invented our own version of Jules Verne's *Michael Strogoff*? At any rate, somewhere between Taganrog and Rostov, the leather trunk containing not just Hermine's trousseau (embroidered at home) but also several Beethoven scores really did vanish.

The engagement ring remained. My grandmother gave it to me on my sixteenth birthday.

Chapter the Ninth. In which, after eleven happy and prosperous years in Rostov, filled with Beethoven and charity projects for Hermine, who set up a school for the children of impoverished Jews, as well as sled races across the endless steppes, followed by tea parties around a humming samovar, the Reinherz family left the city. They were driven away by the "nasty little breeze of anti-Semitism" and several not-so-little pogroms as well. They swapped the Don for the Scheldt River, moving to Antwerp where they raised Julie, Félix, Jenny, and Saloméa, called Selma.

A short epilogue to the "novel" based on André and Simone's relatives on the Reinherz side. This epilogue pertains to the charming small cities in which the ancestors lived, where I have learned that some of my grandmother's more or less distant cousins continued to dwell.

Lemberg (Lviv): possessing, in 1939, a Jewish population of 150,000.

Starved, humiliated, terrorized, tortured, and massacred in situ and inside the Bełżec extermination camp between March 1942 and June 1943. Only a few hundred survivors.

Brody: around 10,000 Jews lived there in 1939.

Likewise, in situ and inside the Bełżec and Majdanek extermination camps.

Only a handful of survivors.

Brzeżany: around 4,000 Jews in 1939.

Likewise, in situ and inside the Bełżec extermination camp, as well as the 10,000 to 12,000 Jews from other small Galician cities penned up in Brzeżany while waiting to be exterminated.

Almost no survivors.

Long ago, as soon as I first began, retrospectively, to be interested in and even attached to my not so distant ancestors' former dwelling places, I instantly happened upon the horrific truth.

I had to say it.

These cities are currently part of Ukraine.

Sterling Ancestors:
From the Alsatian Side

Of course, I must also discuss my Weil, or rather Weill, forebears. They are necessarily less exotic than the Reinherzes. No wolves, no endless steppes, no Cossacks either, just old, peaceful, foursquare Alsace, where Jews were massacred from time to time, but not very often. They were also regularly deported. Only to return later on.

The biggest massacre was in 1349. Then in 1389, an edict banished Jews from the city of Strasbourg. They scattered into the neighboring villages. They were permitted to enter Strasbourg during the daytime, after paying a toll, to sell their wares, mostly livestock and horses, apparently.

The centuries went by, as well as possible, until the French Revolution. On September 27, 1791, Alsatian Jews were proclaimed citizens like all others. Which did not prevent them from being persecuted under the Terror and guillotined unusually often, on various pretexts. Napoleon sorted out all of this.

Nonetheless, I feel that a few interesting chapters might be extracted from the quiet lives of my Weill ancestors, French citizens and residents of Wolfisheim.

Chapter the First. Around 1857, Abraham Weill, André and Simone's grandfather, who was born in 1823 in Wolfisheim, the son of Benjamin Weill, "retailer," and Ghina Gross, and husband of Nanette Lévy, decides to move his family to Strasbourg. Abraham, an ambitious estate agent, has a family of four or five children. Wolfisheim no longer suffices; he requires the big city.

Soon a widower, he would marry Eugénie, Nanette's younger sister. She will give him three more children, including my grandfather Bernard, born in 1872.

Abraham is exceedingly religious, with a wholly Alsatian form of religiousness. No pork or shrimp, naturally. No rice pudding served in plates reserved for meat dishes. Shabbat and Jewish holidays are strictly observed. Yet he never sweeps the pages of an old Talmud with his beard. In the guise of a beard, he sports two colossal sideburns and a neatly trimmed goatee.

Abraham arrives in Strasbourg just in time to witness the major controversy which gripped religious Jews of the day, whether an organ should or could be installed in a synagogue. Those in favor of organs point out that there was one inside the Temple in Jerusalem. Well, a species of organ called a *magrepha*, containing ten holes, each communicating with ten parallel pipes, which made it capable of producing one hundred sounds as a wind instrument. Others, who oppose the organ, remind the congregants that Jews are in mourning since the Destruction of the Temple, and it would be sinful to bring musical instruments into synagogues while this bereavement lasts. They also find it tasteless for synagogues to try to imitate churches. I am not sure with which side of the controversy my grandfather allied himself.

Chapter the Second. In which Alphonse Weill, Abraham's nephew, an eighteen-year-old boy with an appetite for adventure, decides to go see what is happening in America. Disdaining New York and its well-established Jewish communities, he travels to California instead, arriving in July 1870. Three years later, he will open his own store in Bakersfield.

Chapter the Third. Strasbourg has become German territory.

We are in 1871. Abraham, whose business is going well, has a splendid four-story stone house built in the Neustadt quarter.

Nothing is stinted, with square columns, columns with cable molding and lions' heads, stone balconies with sculpted balustrades, two caryatids and two telamons, of which the women are quite bare-breasted, surprisingly, in the home of a religious Jew.

The house resembles its neighbors, which are likewise gems in the Prussian style. But my great-grandfather's house is crowned by a large stone medallion in which the initials AW entwine, for Abraham Weill.

Chapter the Fourth. In which, around 1880, Abraham receives an intriguing letter from his nephew Alphonse. "Come join me, dear Uncle, there are fortunes to be made, California is vast, with more than enough space for the entire Weill family."

Abraham is over fifty. He is unwilling to abandon his lovely house with its lions, columns, and caryatids, without a very good reason. He is proud of his success, and enjoys sleeping at night under the fine stone escutcheon bearing his initials. He rereads Alphonse's letter, then closes his eyes, draws unhurriedly on his long pipe, a splendid white, wide-bowled Alsatian pipe, and decides to send his oldest son, Isidore, twenty years old, as advance man. Isidore is entrusted with deciding if it is suitable for the Weill family to leave its house with caryatids and move to California. My grandfather Bernard is eight years old. At night when he falls asleep, does he sometimes dream of growing up in America?

Meanwhile, one Shabbat follows another and each week, the Weill family, Abraham wearing a bowler hat, Eugénie garbed in all the appropriate furbelows, and the children following them, all walk to the synagogue on the rue Sainte-Hélène (which since 1869 boasts an organ, I am sorry to report). It is quite a walk, but the Weills have strong legs.

Isidore stays away for two years. Then he returns, declaring that America is a materialistic land, devoid of culture, and that the Abraham Weill family of Strasbourg would be unhappy there.

Moving to Paris, Isidore will set up a feather shop.

Nasty gossips in the family claim that Isidore could not have cared less about culture, and that romantic setbacks had put him off America, or rather American women. In this respect, he had been unluckier than Cousin Alphonse, who married pretty, nineteen-year-old Henrietta Lévy in 1882. They will have four children together.

Alphonse also has a dream house built. It is far from the Germanic architectural jewel created for his dear Uncle Abraham. His two-story wooden house is surrounded by several shade-giving porches. Yet it is also a jewel, a jewel of pioneer architecture, as the first house in Bakersfield with a genuine bathroom, which, moreover, is located inside the house.

Chapter the Fifth. In which, during June 1927, Blanche-California Weill, Alphonse's oldest daughter, is found in the office of a Harvard University dean.

The dean pushes up a comfortable armchair, asks Blanche-California to sit down, and tells her more or less the following: "My dear Miss Weill, you defended your dissertation admirably. Tomorrow, a certain number of young men will receive their doctoral degree, in front of their proud families. Can you imagine how humiliating it would be for them to see a young woman receive the very same diploma? My dear Miss Weill, I am appealing to your unselfishness, to your female sensitivity."

He adds, with a friendly smile: "Of course, you can pick up your diploma in my office anytime after tomorrow afternoon."

My cousin Blanche-California, already an adult, has had time to learn that female sensitivity is a trap. She replies politely but firmly that she has every intention of attending the ceremony, where she fully expects to receive her doctorate in science education.

Decades later, she told me this story, while giving me a tour of San Francisco.

I checked the Harvard diploma records and found that my cousin was possibly not the only young woman to receive a doctorate that year from the university. Someone boasting the first name Psyche is listed among the graduates, and I cannot believe that

Psyche was a young man. Might my cousin Blanche-California's story be unreliable? Or had Psyche, a shy flower, more submissive than Alphonse's daughter, decided long beforehand to drop the idea of attending the ceremony, and to wait obediently for her diploma to be mailed to her?

Some chapters follow which lack serious literary interest. Abraham's descendants will leave Strasbourg for Paris, they will multiply, and succeed in business, while others will advance in the arts. Bernard's sisters will regret that instead of marrying an Alsatian or at least a woman from the Lorraine, their brother chose a *Galitzianerin*. They took comfort by claiming that it was a question of dowry, and a young doctor must settle down. Selma despised them and never encouraged Simone and André to see their uncles, aunts, and cousins. The Weill family complained: "We hardly know those children."

Without further ado, we skip ahead to Chapter the Twentieth. In which we find the entire city of Bakersfield celebrating the ninety-ninth birthday of Lawrence, the son of Alphonse. It is May 14, 1988, which has been declared "Lawrence Weill Day."

That is because the California Weills were extremely rich and gave generously to charity. A far cry, however, from the modest grandmothers in Brody and Lemberg handing out food and clothing. This is America, land of large-scale philanthropy. Henrietta Weill and her daughters opened free pediatric clinics and bankrolled several foundations. Blanche-California established clinics for "discouraged children." Lawrence was the last survivor of a family who had so greatly helped modernize the insular small town to which Alphonse the Alsatian had moved in 1873.

I am absolutely sure that this oh-so-American fete included a brass band, fireworks, speeches, and the letting loose of multicolored helium balloons. My near-centenarian cousin was driven through the streets in a Cadillac convertible, and showered with confetti.

I so wish I had been there!

Alphonse's home, the Weill House, donated in 1950 to the

Kern County Museum, along with its porches and bathroom, is still included among Bakersfield's tourist landmarks.

This chapter also has a postscript.

Through a peculiar historical irony, more than sixty years after his invitation to Uncle Abraham—which was refused because of culture and the Germanic architectural jewel—in 1942 old Alphonse got Bernard, Selma, and Simone out of France. He paid the astronomical sums demanded by shipping companies to transport Jewish refugees. He, along with Blanche-California, signed all the guarantees and affidavits required to obtain American visas, promised to house, feed, and take care of the whole family forever, if need be. Thanks to him, there were some linen and bedcovers for my cradle, and true to his word, he paid for the sanatorium when my mother had a relapse of tuberculosis shortly after I was born.

He did not save Simone, no one could save her, but he almost certainly saved my grandparents from deportation and horrible deaths.

The Wages of Sin

THE TIME MAY HAVE COME FOR ME TO ADMIT THAT I AM AN abominable hypocrite, and despite my indignation over the "advantages" which, in Simone's view, baptism might have brought me, as well as the drawbacks of life as a relic, sometimes I have readily traded Simone for worldly advantages which she would have despised, as I am wholly aware.

The first time I spent a full academic year in New York, to teach at the Lycée Français, I rented a room on the Upper West Side, in a sort of dormitory which was nicknamed The Wages of Sin. The twelve-story building towered over neighboring houses, and the landlords had painted the exposed south wall, a windowless wall, to depict an enormous Bible page with the inscription in huge letters: "The Wages of Sin Is Death." This gigantic page with its quote was visible from afar, to anyone heading up Broadway.

It was a fairly gloomy place which, I sometimes felt during the eight or ten months I lived there, would have pleased my aunt (although perhaps not as a stopover place for me, her "Patapon," whom she condemned to middle-class normality). It swarmed with sad, lonely people whose dreams led nowhere, and emigrants who cooked strange vittles in their rooms. The whole place smelt of curry and burnt lard. One night, two people from who knows where asphyxiated themselves in their room, and for an entire week, the bleak odor of gas drifted through the elevator and hall-ways. But I am getting ahead of myself.

My second-floor room was foul and especially dark. Twenty-four hours after I moved in, I was intrigued by shouts and singing from the ground floor, and went downstairs to the lobby. There, a dozen people formed a circle, with their arms stretched upward, more or less in a trance, praying to Jesus. Among them, and not the least exalted, were the dormitory's landladies, two Swedish-born sisters, dressed in long white robes with their long gray hair awry. I had moved in with the members of a highly active mystical sect and, in the following months, would often see them pray to the Lord late at night, wearing capacious white nightgowns. The very next day, I started a conversation with the two sisters. I explained that I was the niece of Simone Weil. They had heard of my aunt and almost embraced me in joy and amazement. Delighted by their re-action, I shamelessly asked them if they had a better room for me. Two days later, I brought them a half-dozen Swedish translations of my aunt's books, taken from my father's office at Princeton, and I moved into a light-filled studio on the eleventh floor, with a fine Hudson River view. For the rest of my stay with them, the two sisters treated me with consideration and respect.

Even so, my graduation to the upper spheres of The Wages of Sin was followed by some nights filled with horror, bewilderment, and panic. It was the first time I had ever slept on a mattress in-fested with bedbugs, and I did not realize at first what was hap-pening. Surely it was a punishment from heaven. I had to buy a new bed. I think that even Simone would not have stood for it. Bedbugs are truly atrocious.

A Family Unglued

THE DAY AFTER MY MOTHER DIED, PEOPLE CAME UP TO US TO offer their condolences. Since I was unknown to them, my father introduced me: "My sister, Simone."

It was surely due to emotion and grief. Yet that same confusion dated back many years.

Was I not, even as a baby, intended to replace Simone in the view of her family? The one bequeathed by her to them?

During the weeks which preceded her departure from New York, she talked endlessly about me. And up to her final letter, which they would receive several days after learning of her death: *Darlings, very little time or inspiration available for letters now. They will be brief, few and far-between. But you have another source of comfort.*

"Our poor little Simonette loved us so much," said my weeping grandfather after André, accompanied by Doctor Bercher, brought my grandparents the telegram announcing Simone's death.

Was it because of the "She never wanted you to know" added by Zette Closon to the telegram? Biri knew that only he and Mime could have cured their daughter, saving her yet again from her furious urge for self-destruction. He knew that she could not survive without them.

Had Bernard realized at that moment that the letters which for months had delighted him and Selma were just a long succession of lies?

The lovely descriptions of London in springtime, work, strolls, and Simone's new friends were but fiction, intended to hoodwink her unfortunate parents. The only true element in all these letters is the baby with a sunny smile, over whom she cast a spell, as she boasts, the baby to whom she always, even in telegrams, sends her "fondest kisses," writing the words in English.

On the day that Zette Closon's telegram arrived, Mime spoke of killing herself. André never forgave her for it. After all, he was still alive.

This was the first fissure.

The family, which had been so close-knit until Simone's death, would soon come apart. Not immediately. My mother was obliged to stay at a Pennsylvania sanatorium. My grandparents took me in to live with them in New York, on Riverside Drive, and for six or eight months, devoted all their energy, intelligence, and affection to me. Mime's letters to Eveline consist of long "reports" about the "princess," my teething, my physical prowesses, what I eat and drink, my growing feet. Mime fashions shoes for me, Biri goes out to buy me a waterproof cape, Mime sews clothes for me, and Biri installs special fencing on the fire escape so that I can enjoy the fresh air at any time. Both get up at dawn to take me for a walk when it is still cool, my vocabulary is developing, I know how to count and identify colors, whether cousin Blanche-California, with her doctorate in science education, likes it or not. Now working with discouraged children in New York, she claims that children can identify colors only at age three and older. I am a darling, adorable, I comfort my grandmother who finds it hilarious when I throw her eyeglasses out the window, I am a precious bundle of joy who brings merriment to her grandfather: *Biri laughed so much . . .*

Naturally, Mime's letters are full of affection for Eveline, since she is far away. Mime wishes her a quick recovery, but in the meantime, the baby with the sunny smile, the source of comfort, belongs to Mime and Biri.

They will soon be fighting over the unfortunate source of comfort, who will become a little hostage, shunted among four adults who are out of control: André and Eveline, Bernard and Selma.

The first clash will occur in February 1945 on the ship *Rio Tunuyan*, which is carrying the whole family from New Orleans to Brazil. Mime constantly keeps me on her lap, and forbids me to go near another little girl named Patty, whom she considers dirty. André tears me out of his mother's arms and hands me over, a screaming toddler, to Eveline. Biri calls André a stinker and tells him that I am Mime's and his last joy in life. Eveline locks herself up with me in her cabin, where I spend three days screaming that I want Mime. Eveline finds this unpleasant and will hold it against me for the rest of her life. Once I have calmed down, and grown accustomed to the substitution, I am returned to my grandparents. Eveline is feeling tired.

The years spent in Brazil are peaceful. They are years of survival, anticipating a potential return to Europe. The whole family struggles to adapt to a difficult climate. Bernard writes to his cousin Alphonse in California: *Since she came here, our little Sylvie coughs and suffers from enteritis. In New York, we were told that the São Paulo climate is ideal! When we tell that to people here, they fall down laughing. And apparently, no one ever gets used to it!*

I often stay with my grandparents. I am their reason for living. And it is practical for my parents.

The war is over. My sister is born. At the end of 1947, Mime and Biri move to Switzerland, and we go to Chicago, where my father has been appointed professor. In the spring of 1948, I have a serious primary tuberculosis infection and my grandparents take me to live with them in Switzerland. The following year, the whole family reunites on the rue Auguste-Comte.

In 1952, I believe, begins the long series of squabbles, fallings-out, lawsuits, truces, settlements, and fresh fallings-out which would endure for the remainder of my childhood and beyond, until Selma's death in November 1965.

A location exists which symbolizes in my memory this endless family nightmare, the narrow stairway which connected the big sixth-floor apartment to the seventh-floor studio. During the years when my parents and grandparents were on good terms, the door at the foot of the cramped staircase was open, and my sister and I would sleep on the sixth floor, or I would sleep there by myself. The big apartment was part of our landscape, where we played cards with Biri, and ate Mime's wonderful butter cookies. The years during which the adults only communicated through lawyers, the door was locked on both sides, and we used the stairway as a clothes closet and storage space. As a teenager, I spent hours sitting on the steps, listening to the noises which rose from the sixth floor, the sounds of Mime's life: her heavy step in the corridor, her voice when she welcomed visitors, her interjections and laughter. Hearing her laugh was what hurt me most.

Naturally, at the core of the dispute was the one who was gone, Simone, and what she had left behind. To begin with, there was me, the baby whom she had bequeathed to her parents. Bernard and Selma would have wanted to raise me, or at least share me with my parents. Wrong or right, my father felt that his mother had made Simone dependent upon her, and Simone died because of this dependence. He was intent on eliminating in me this "need for Mime" which he construed as harmful.

Quite soon the dispute extended to Simone's manuscripts. My grandparents threw themselves into getting them published. My father, feeling that no one had been closer to his sister than himself, expressed his will to play a role in each publication. Nothing would happen without his approval and involvement. My grandparents (and later my grandmother alone, after my grandfather's death in 1955) did not see things the same way. They wanted to donate all the manuscripts to the Bibliothèque Nationale. My father was against this, as long as they had not been published in their entirety. They wanted to bequeath them to the BN, but my father objected, reminding them that he was a joint heir.

For some years, a "kidnapping" of manuscripts went on. Deposited at the Bibliothèque Nationale by my grandparents, they were later brought back to the rue Auguste-Comte, and then returned to the BN, by André, only to be clamored for by Selma, who took them back, accusing André of having suddenly absconded with them early one morning: *I heard an intruder in my home. Worried, I got up and found, in Simone's room, my son busy piling into a suitcase all the manuscripts and transcripts which I had been working on all summer long. Despite my protests, he took them away, refusing to give me a list. He claims to have deposited them at the Bibliothèque Nationale.* In this way, the manuscripts, or some of them, made several round trips between the BN and the rue AC.

When did Bernard and Selma conceive the notion of bequeathing their apartment to the Bibliothèque Nationale for it to be transformed into a Simone Weil Museum? The BN had no intention of opening a museum on the rue Auguste-Comte, but did not discourage my grandparents from pursuing their project, so they had wills drawn up accordingly. Aged and embittered, they declared André and his family unworthy of occupying the place where Simone had lived.

They had filled the apartment with the silent presence of Simone. André was too lively and demanding, while the little girls were too noisy and hectic, and Eveline too fragrant. André might have defused the situation by living elsewhere with his family during their stays in Paris. But no, the Weils clung to the rue Auguste-Comte like mussels on a rock.

At the time, did anyone grasp the terrible sadness of this four-way divorce? Did anyone try to placate the humiliated son, who reacted angrily to his parents' public maneuvers to disinherit him, or the two elderly parents, badly influenced and advised, obsessed with keeping alive the memory of their dead daughter?

To my knowledge, one man did, the doctor Louis Bercher, who was dismayed by what he called a "distressing conflict among people who are all good people."

Simone had already been transformed into a saint, and Selma into the saint's mother. In this scheme, André was necessarily the devil. My father's hot-tempered nature did not help matters. Well-known personalities in the Parisian intellectual world sought for years to inflame the strife, to exploit the grief of an unsettled family which was making itself look ridiculous. I cannot validate either side's case. I can only say that in Simone's name, they all often managed to give my childhood years a bitter taste.

One day when I was eleven, studying at the Lycée Montaigne, Biri waited for me when school was let out. That winter I was living with my maternal grandmother, since my parents and sister were in Chicago. It was a year during which my parents and grandparents were not on speaking terms. Four times a day, I walked past the building on the rue Auguste-Comte, but did not go up to my grandparents' apartment. My father had instructed me: "If you run into them, be polite, but do not dawdle." I must have seen them once or twice from afar, walking slowly arm-in-arm, looking alike in their dark old raincoats and berets, yet it seemed that they were not really Mime and Biri, butter cookies and *croquignoles*, but two strangers, two villains who had thrown out my mother, sister, and me the summer before, while André was away from home. I think this occurred in response to a harsh letter which he had written to the Bibliothèque Nationale, which was forwarded in turn to my grandparents.

And suddenly on a dreary winter afternoon, there was Biri, only a few meters away, looking at me silently, almost shyly, and I saw heavy tears flowing down his cheeks into his moustache, now white and sparser. Like him, I stood rooted to the spot for a few seconds, holding my school bag, looking at him, unsure of what to do. I did not run towards him to kiss him. I nodded slightly, and quickly walked away. I have never, ever forgiven myself.

He died the following year. We saw him one last time, gaunt

and exhausted. After this latest bereavement, a truce followed for about one year. Then everything started up again, with renewed intensity.

The Metamorphoses
of a Kuckucksei

ACCORDING TO A FAMILY STORY, SELMA LAUGHINGLY BOASTED of having played the *Internationale* on a piano in the lounge of a big hotel in the mountains, where the four Weils were spending a few days on vacation, soon after World War I. After several guests complained, the hotel's manager sent a maid over to ask her to stop this indecent display. Selma's in-laws were at least as appalled as the rich hotel guests, and fifty years later, they still spoke of the incident.

Was the mother of André and Simone a bit of a troublemaker?

During her long life, my grandmother Selma underwent a certain number of transformations. A histrionic character if ever there was one, capable of slipping into various roles and acting them perfectly, she was only known to me in her last two roles. Firstly, during my early childhood, that of bereaved mother, although looking after me, her granddaughter, with maternal love and tireless self-sacrifice. For example, in 1944, during a sweltering New York summer, she refused an offer from our rich cousin Blanche-California Weill of two weeks' vacation in the country, for fear that in a hotel, her "princess" (me, as a baby) could not spend the whole day in the bathtub, the only pastime which pleased me that summer. She enfolded me in a magical protective cocoon, as she had done for her children, and I adored her. Then, as the years went on, I saw her ripen into her last role, the glorious and uncanny role of Saint's mother.

It happened on the rue Auguste-Comte, in the apartment transformed into a kind of temple with the holy of holies, Simone's room, at the end of the corridor. As you entered, to the right was the shipping trunk covered with a doily, the big photo, the vase filled with flowers. The long wooden table, the neatly arranged books on light wood shelves which had never belonged to Simone, her *Collection Budé*, Gregorian Missal, and a complete set of the novels of Rétif de la Bretonne. At a given time, Simone had thought that by reading the latter, she might acquire some knowledge about the facts of life, or so my father explained in a half-mocking, half-serious tone which also contained a touch of admiration, as if the odd plan of learning about life from Rétif were yet another arcane sign of the "*trollesse's*" superiority. He always spoke about his sister in this manner.

My grandmother, garbed in dark, unfeminine woolen garments, her head covered by a black lace mantilla which fell onto her shoulders, elongating her face and giving her a vaguely religious appearance, her lips stretched into a wide, painful smile, would welcome Simone's admirers, lavishing affection upon them and insisting that they call her Mime.

Although she had never wanted to be called Mom or Grandma before, now when she gave her own handwritten transcripts of her daughter's texts to friends, she signed them "Simone's mom."

Although previously she had loathed churchy people, now she kept up a mystical, sentimental correspondence with a small circle of clergymen. The latter, who became regular visitors at the rue Auguste-Comte, were also regularly haunted by visions of Simone. She walked alongside them and accompanied them, they were sure of it, and her presence was infused with a highly pure and tender friendship for them. One or another of these followers wrote: "Not a single day goes by without my turning to her, and silently consulting her."

They would shut themselves up with Selma inside Simone's room. When they were far away, they would write to her. Of course, I only read this correspondence much later.

They call my grandmother "my very dear Mime." They declare that Simone lives again through her, that few mothers are as fulfilled as she, dearest Mime who for so many years has lived only with, through, and for her daughter. They tell her that Simone has immortalized her. They say: "You and Simone are the same person." They declare that it would be unbearable to lose her, because that would mean losing Simone again. She is a "true manifestation" of Simone.

And then her correspondents always kiss her tenderly, as well as respectfully of course, with respectful tenderness, with tender respect. The valedictions vary, suggesting a fear of appearing repetitive.

Simone's mom also kisses them tenderly, and even with all her tender affection. She rediscovers the girlish sentimental tone of the letters which gushed from her during her teens, as well as those she wrote to Mademoiselle Chaintreuil, her children's schoolteacher, who became a great friend and confidant.

Well done, Mime! In retrospect, today I feel proud of you. Why not, during the rather sad last years of your life, why not, at over eighty, indulge in these little ecclesiastical flirtations, so pleasant and flattering, with their stream of tender and respectful kisses, with all those: I am with you, You are with me, Simone is with us, and We are together in Simone . . . ?

Still, at the time, not only was I not proud of you, but I wholeheartedly loathed the cockroaches who swarmed and groveled at your feet, whispering, muttering Simone's name like a mantra which they used to invade my territory. At age ten, I had read *Tartuffe*, and I despised the tubby priests whom you invited to lunch, who blissfully sat down to eat your choucroute, devouring chunks of meat even on Fridays, claiming that everything is allowed while traveling.

To think that poor Simone had written her most sincere and despairing pages to these hypocrites. Now they were in possession of dear Mime and her choucroute.

The cockroaches had taken all the space, and there was scarcely any left for us. The Saint's mom was so engrossed by her duties that she no longer really wanted to be a grandmother. The ecclesiastical flirtations wove a web of sainthood around the woman whom they called Mime, permanently separating her from us, her family. Making her into a stranger.

This stranger was born in Rostov-on-Don. She had been named Saloméa in memory of her grandfather Salomon Sternberg, who died shortly before she was born. Little Saloméa, called Selma, was a nihilist at the age of two-and-a-half years, according to her brother, and by age seven was frightfully liberated, if a close relative can be believed. Perhaps affectionately, Hermine gave her the unflattering nickname *Kuckucksei*. The cuckoo's egg, the egg which fell from elsewhere, who knows where, thrown randomly into the nest and destined to cause nothing but trouble and vexation to those around her. She would keep this nickname.

It might be necessary to describe the Reinherz family's life in Antwerp, in a spacious house filled with music, governed by Hermine, a highly proper and domineering mother. She often repeats to her daughters: "A young lady never has an opinion," even after they are over twenty years old. Their father, Adolphe Grigorievitch, is showing his age, and divides his days between his grain business and Hebrew poetry. Their beloved son Félix, the family's luminary, an accomplished violinist at age eighteen, studies law at the University of Brussels, and is also a talented draughtsman. The three golden-voiced daughters are also fine pianists, and ideal future homemakers, of course.

How do I know all this? Because this is a family that always writes everything down. Hermine Solomonovna routinely travels to visit her large family in Vienna and Paris. After 1893, she is accompanied by her oldest daughter, Julie, an eligible bride. During each absence, she demands a four-page letter in French or German from everyone who remained at home. Félix suggests publishing these letters under the title "Letters from an Intelligent Family."

As a teenager, Selma writes letters displaying a violently passionate nature, champing at the bit with impatience and boredom. Having finished school at around fifteen, her main activities were in the household, while her beloved brother led the exalting and eventful life of a student.

Selma still had music. And diction lessons.

Dear Mama, I can hear you saying: "She has found a new hobby-horse!" But it is really serious, even a real passion. My friend Céleste says that our diction teacher, who dined with them on Wednesday, sang my praises persistently! You can imagine how ecstatic that made me. I beg you to never believe Félix's jokes. The things he says about me! That's because he does not have enough subject matter to fill four pages.

This passion for diction plainly concurs with a taste for the theater. At sixteen, Selma liked to play at being a well-dressed lady who goes on outings, wearing an elegant hat. Félix, the older brother whom she worshipped, was protective towards his younger sisters, whom he called his "little kids," and played along, mockingly:

In town, people are very amused at the sight of my sister putting on airs as she does her shopping. She claims that everyone sees her as a young woman going out with her husband. The husband is Yours truly! Setting out to buy two anchovy fillets, she accomplishes the feat of going into Locus's shop and eating two pastries, ditto at Lenz's shop, then buying a roquefort cheese, and finally forgetting all about the anchovy fillets. That is why, on a day like today, when I have the pleasure of taking a walk with her, we are seen going back and forth along the rue des Tanneurs, the pont de Meir, and the Marché aux Souliers no fewer than thirty-six times. Thanks to which we encounter over fifty of my school friends, and Mademoiselle is ecstatic.

Then comes the tragedy. In November 1895, Félix, aged twenty, dies of typhoid fever. The Reinherz family goes to stay a while in a Brussels hotel. After their return to Antwerp, they can no longer stand their house, so they resolve to move. Adolphe Reinherz, elderly and taciturn, will never get over his son's death.

The following springtime, Hermine goes traveling with Julie again, still seeking a husband for her. The requirement for family members who stay at home remains four pages daily. The family correspondence continues on black-bordered mourning stationery, but Félix is never mentioned again.

Instead we find Selma painstakingly reassuring, and verbosely assembling details to momentarily amuse, her poor bereaved mother.

Seeing that my hat had suffered from its stay in the countryside at Westerloo, I completely removed the trimmings and undertook the arduous task of retrimming the hat. You know how patient I am, so soon I was in darkest despair, and I wept amid the scraps of tulle, gauze, and lace, as did Marius (or if not him, somebody else) upon the ruins of Carthage.

I was busy making my headgear during all of yesterday afternoon and evening. This morning, after chatting with Daddy, making the beds, darning stockings, stitching buttons (unbelievable but nevertheless true), I had my lesson with Miss Adams.

A few days later:

Dear Mama and dear Juleke, I am working like a slave, in the literal as well as figurative sense, since I am black from dust, just like a New Zealand native.

Today I put the greenhouse in order, did three baskets of laundry, tidied up, dusted, and scrubbed the second-floor bedrooms. Tell me again that I am not on the point of becoming an ideal homemaker. Yet another medal to add to those which already decorate my bosom.

Ardent declarations of love almost always follow:

If one day the unlikely should occur, and in the distant future I get married, I could never feel for any husband the passionate affection which I feel for you, nor the blind confidence which I have in you. Farewell, dear, dear Mama, I send you thousands and thousands of kisses.

The above is true, authentic Selma. For her whole life, she would be the great specialist in declarations of undivided, passionate affection, involving thousands and thousands of kisses. To her two children, her husband, and me.

After she is married, Selma will continue the tradition begun by her mother. The four Weils will write one another incessantly. Selma is almost as demanding as Hermine, and no sooner has she received a letter than she requires another one. One day Simone will rebel: *There is one mistake above all to be avoided in my case, which would be to think that I am a darling,* she writes from Italy (she was twenty-eight or twenty-nine years old) in response to a letter in which Selma tells her to be a darling and write back immediately. Simone then adds: *In the past five days, I have sent two letters and a telegram. This seems to me more than enough . . . If this goes on, having to write all the time will spoil the fun of traveling.*

As for me, when I was seven or eight years old, I was amazed and outraged because Mime's replies to my letters always ended with something like: *It would be so nice if you wrote to us . . .*

Stylish Selma, who had been the perfect homemaker at age seventeen, will plan an entirely different education for her daughter. The latter will not fill her days by making hats. Selma aims to make her into some kind of boy.

In June 1914 she writes to her dear friend Mademoiselle Chaintreuil, *I am doing my best to nurture a boy's uprightness in Simone, instead of a little girl's charm, even if it winds up seeming like rudeness.*

For she loathes little girls and their *little poses and pouts in the presence of company.*

I was repeatedly told about the following incident, known in the family as the "famous visit to the tailor." Selma and her sister-in-law took fifteen-year-old Simone and her cousin Raymonde to the family tailor. The two girls proceeded to try on skirts and overcoats. Simone let herself be dressed, but refused to look in the mirror. She was begged to please glance at it, just to see if she was satisfied with the tailor's work. Simone obstinately looked to one side.

"Mademoiselle is entirely wrapped up in her studies," said the tailor, who was a diplomat.

Was Simone afraid to see herself as pretty? Did she already believe what she would later jot down in a notebook, that a pretty woman who looks in the mirror might believe that she is nothing more than that?

What about Selma? On that afternoon, did she feel elated or troubled? Was that what she had planned? Yet she does up her daughter rather stylishly. A class photo shows Simone at around age thirteen, in a pretty dress, with tousled, but neatly cut, hair.

Just what sort of mother had the *Kuckucksei* been? I believe she was a mother full of contradictions. To begin with, she had been a proud and concerned mother wolf, never letting her children out of her sight for a second.

My major ambition, my major desire for my children's future is not that they be useful, or good, or intelligent, but that they be happy! I am doubtless expressing myself poorly, but all the same, maternal love basically contains a lot of selfishness. It is an almost animal need to keep her little ones from suffering!

With André, she certainly gets her wish. In June 1914, she writes: *With André, I have the clear impression that he may be influenced but not directed, as his personality is too pronounced for that. I am doubtless wrong to worry, since at present he has a happy nature which provides him sensual pleasures at every moment, and there is no reason he should not be equally happy later on.*

My father is already a sensualist at age eight!

And already busy doing math, as Selma writes in December 1914: *Starting this past summer, he has had a real passion for geometry. He got hold of one of his older cousin's schoolbooks* (Geometry by Émile Borel) *and I cannot tell you the ardor and joy with which he studies this volume and draws diagrams. I lack the courage to deprive him of this pleasure, even though the subject is surely beyond his age level.*

By contrast, Simone is giving her the runaround. From June 1914: *Nothing is to be done as long as her nasty mood persists. She cannot be reasoned with, or calmed down with affectionate words, nor made to obey by adopting a severe tone. I have certainly spoiled her.*

Simonette is a genuine little woman and is wonderfully able to use her charm, when she feels like it.

Selma seems to suffer from self-doubt. She has not yet succeeded in making Simone into a boy, and is equally unable to make her into a genuine, docile little girl.

From July 1914: *I am spending all my time preventing Simone from letting herself be wooed by young men! She has lots of success with them, which delights her, but I can no longer stand to see these young men flatter and caress her . . . So I am forced to constantly monitor this budding flirt, who despite my forbiddance, never misses a chance to chat with her worshippers!*

Remarkably, in one of her last letters to her parents, the former five-year-old "budding flirt" revisits this theme of detrimental admirers: *I beg you, protect her from exchanging smiles with admirers! I assure you that her personality is already starting to form. This delectable little one may very well turn into a selfish, heartless being (while remaining delectable). These thoughts may be painful, but we owe it to her to not just enjoy her.*

The delectable little one was me. I was not yet one year old.

Simone's biographers describe the rotten pranks played by Simone and André. They went to beg sweets from the neighbors, claiming that they were dying of hunger, or went out to walk in midwinter wearing sandals without socks, until their teeth chattered and passersby would shout abuse at their mother. Mime laughed heartily at these pranks, and was still laughing when she told me about them fifty years later. Yet it seemed to me that these pranks were designed to make her look like a bad mother. Did André and Simone find her too perfect, suffocatingly so?

How many times did I hear André say that he went to teach in India partly to escape? He would add:

"Simone could never flee anywhere. Except at the end, of course."

My grandmother often gave the impression of being onstage. When she entered a room, she filled it with her presence. When she left it, the room suddenly seemed empty.

Her writings also shared this theatrical quality. We might also simply say that she overdid things. Yes, Selma always overdid things a little, to better conform to the role which she was playing at the moment.

This dated back to her teenage years. In May 1896, when she was seventeen, Selma writes this truly unexpected letter to her mother:

Despite your fears, Gertrud is behaving very well, and I am getting along with her very well, that is to say she receives the two or three words which I address to her during the day with the respect due to my abilities and inarguable dignity. I think you can rest easy about her, and my term in office will be characterized by the most perfect calm. I would find it just as hard to speak condescendingly to the maids as I would to speak with them about anything except the menu, or work to be done. I cannot understand how one can inform servants about things which touch one personally, as so many people do. I would find it impossible to hold a conversation with a maid, and I feel a perhaps excessive repulsion towards all people of that category.

Can a more loathsome "bourgeoise" be imagined? Is Selma being sincere? Or is she overdoing it to please her mother? Around the same time, she laments that she is only a *Kuckucksei* who never does anything right. It is hard to believe that this is the same Selma who will play the *Internationale* in a fancy hotel. The same who will be delighted to see her daughter, then aged sixteen, gather all the maids in the garden of the Hôtel du Château at Challes-les-Eaux one night and advise them to unionize. The same one who, in December 1931, will write proudly from Le Puy to André, who was then teaching at Aligarh, India:

Now I am going to tell you about the unbelievable "canulars" which are being played here. Last Thursday a delegation of unemployed men was supposed to visit the mayor. No compensation for the unemployed had been voted in this godforsaken place. They were merely allowed to break rocks at six francs per cubic meter on a large square in front of the lycée. Suddenly, the "trollesse" decided to take matters in hand, given the reticence of the proletariat in this lair of churchgoers. She offered to join the delegation, and they accepted enthusiastically . . . As the police detective at Le Puy showed her, an official file is recording everything she has done (the editor of Le Puy's sole quasi-left-wing newspaper told her that two stool pigeons among the unemployed immediately went to the police station to report everything). This file states, among other things, that after a town council meeting, she went to buy drinks for some of the unemployed in a café (which is strictly true, and it may even be assumed that the stool pigeons were among them, which is especially funny), and that the next day she shook hands (!!) with two unemployed men on the square in front of the lycée, that she was carrying a copy of L'Humanité at the time, etc. There was also a complaint from the Parent Teacher Association.

In short, you see that your soror amply deserves your congratulations.

Now Selma has slipped into another role, a fairly noble but unsettled one, as mother of a "trollesse"-professor-union organizer, mother of the woman whom the right-wing press, echoing some of Simone's teachers at the École Normale, nicknames the "Red Virgin."

Yet Selma has also not quite given up as a middle-class mother. During this same stay at Le Puy, she writes to Bernard: No, you see, I think she is unmarriageable! Naturally, she writes that with a smile, as many mothers do. Simone is not yet twenty-three years old; she still has time to become marriageable, or so her mother still believes.

At almost the same time, she replies to André, who has just announced that he has made a mathematical discovery (after she writes to Bernard, informing him that she wept with joy upon learning the news): Nothing on earth can cause me more joy than what you tell us about your work, and I congratulate you from the bottom of my heart for the "birth" which you have announced. What a great feeling it must be to discover something new!

Yet what did this mother of the Red Virgin genuinely hope for? What did she want for her children? In December 1931 she sent the following New Year wishes to her beloved and brilliant "kid," who had fled his too-perfect mother as far as India:

I am joyfully looking forward to the year 1932, thinking that it will bring you back to us. Receive all my wishes, darling, you know that your happiness and Simone's are our only hope and our only ambition.

When all is said and done, the wolf mother will always emerge and persist, until the end. The female wolf who, even after becoming the Saint's mom, would nonetheless sigh repeatedly: "I would have so much preferred a happy life for her!"

These Ruined Faces

Simone, I love you!

This is how a New York lecture ended a few years ago. It was a lecture notable for its sensitive and intriguing insights into Simone Weil's trajectory, winding up with this declaration of love, provoked by a long—and bloody, as I recall—description of the Virgin in labor, giving birth to Jesus.

As for me, my darling (recall that we write this way within the family), my brilliant aunt, my sainted aunt, there are days, even many of them, when I truly do not love you.

Think for a moment about the inheritance which you left me. You bequeathed a ruined family to me. You left me the tears of your parents—whom I naturally called Mime and Biri, as you and André had always called them—your parents who raised me in part, and whose usual expression was despair. I rarely saw them smile, except perhaps sadly. I almost never saw them laugh wholeheartedly, with joy.

The "source of comfort" which you left them was only a baby, who did not have the strength to bear the weight of such despair. Nevertheless, it seems that I fulfilled my duties as a consoling baby to the best of my ability. How do I know that? Listen to what Mime said, or rather wrote, one year after your death, while I was living with my grandparents in the Riverside Drive apartment where you had also lived: *I do everything I can to avoid crying in front of her, but when it happens, she notices right away and runs over to caress me and say "love" with such an adorable smile that your heart melts on seeing it.*

I do not remember any of that.

But I do recall, as one of my first memories, Biri's tears flowing into his moustache, and from there onto my forehead.

I am sitting in his lap; we are surely in his São Paulo apartment, where I also lived with them. I am on Biri's lap, and he is showing me a shiny square of paper upon which I recognize him, even though his hair and moustache seem too dark. He is seated on an armchair in a garden, and he is holding a little girl in his lap, exactly the way he is holding me. I happily exclaim: "That is Biri!" My grandfather, pointing to the photo, replies in a trembling voice: "And that is my little girl. You look like her." I feel his damp moustache against my cheek. I think, No, I am his little girl! At first, I do not understand. But he shows me the photo often, and soon I will grasp that I have a double and the fact that this double exists, on a dog-eared old photo, makes my grandfather weep.

So to make him stop crying, I had to tell him: "Bounce me up and down, sing '*Hoppe, hoppe, Reiter*'!"

Many decades have gone by, but I still feel heartbroken when I look at Mime and Biri's distraught, blank old faces in the photos on their passports, visas, and residents' permits. Gray, as if drained of blood, and their eyes painfully dull.

These old people will trudge from continent to continent, North America to South America, Brazil to Switzerland, one place to another, where they have nothing to do and their only duty is to take care of me. Yet in truth, I do not replace their "Simonette."

You have bequeathed these ruined faces to me, these tears, and these last letters in which they speak to you as one speaks to an adored child. Your father sends you prescriptions for anti-migraine pills, and he jokes, as is his custom: *We have everything we need, especially since we are both earning heaps of dough. What do you say to that? Me, a professor! Now we've seen everything!* Your mother worries about whether you are comfortably attired for the summer heat, and advises you to eat properly. They tell you about me, and you reply that you are fine and that you never tire of getting details about "Sylvie with the sunny smile." You are in the process of letting yourself die.

It was not as if you left them against your own wishes. As if you had been deported or shot. It is not an everyday bereavement when a daughter absolutely insists on destroying herself, and then succeeds.

They barely spoke about the war, emigration, exile, the extermination of six million Jews, including some close relatives transported from Drancy to Auschwitz by convoy 67 on February 3, 1944. It was as if bereavement for an entire vanished world were condensed and gathered into a single grief, their mourning over you.

One month before you died, you wrote that only your parents could "glue" you "back together again." Your death made your family come unglued permanently. Our life was spent unglued.

The Garde-Meuble

WHILE MY GRANDPARENTS WERE TRANSCRIBING, MY PARENTS
went to a place known as the *garde-meuble*.*

This term was often used as part of the family vocabulary. I can
still hear the way it was said by my father and mother. My father
asked: "Are you planning to go to the *garde-meuble* today?" My
mother would inform us: "I went to the *garde-meuble* this morning." It seemed like the *garde-meuble* was a place where adults often went, like the dentist's office or hair salon. Either my mother
went to have tea at a friend's home, or she went to the *garde-meuble*. Or she did both, one after the other. I had no idea what could
possibly be in a *garde-meuble*, since the word *meuble*† vanished in
the composite word, losing its concrete meaning, which was well
known to me. When we were in Paris, we lived in a vast, gloomy
apartment devoid of furniture, and my parents stopped off at a
place called the *garde-meuble*. What did they do there? This was
a mystery.

*Translator's note: A *garde-meuble* is a storage unit.
†Translator's note: *Meuble* means "furniture."

116

What could have possibly remained in the *garde-meuble*, since the Germans took everything? I later learned what was there: books and clothes, especially those which André wore in India, where he enjoyed being mistaken for a young Kashmiri gentleman. There were also vacation souvenirs, piled up at random in old trunks, and some worthless furniture which had belonged to my mother's family. All this disheartening paraphernalia entered the rue Auguste-Comte in 1965, after Selma died.

It took me a long time to realize that my parents were hoping to return to France permanently, which would have allowed them to transfer whatever was in the *garde-meuble* into their very own apartment, whether in Paris or Strasbourg.

This permanent return never occurred.

My father was accused of cowardice for not having joined the army in September 1939. It was written that Simone, who elsewhere was so keen on sacrifice and heroism, had accepted, aided, and abetted her brother's "cowardice." It was not a matter of cowardice. She accepted and abetted the fact that like her, he was animated by the passion to fulfill what he considered his mission in life. One might reply that mathematics is not vital for mankind's well-being, and that just when Hitler was about to invade France, other things were more urgent. This point of view can be plausibly argued. The terribly nearsighted André was convinced of his uselessness as an infantry lieutenant, and his great usefulness as a mathematician. In 1936, the equally nearsighted Simone had already gone to "fight the war" in Spain, where she demanded to be issued a rifle. Since she was unable to aim, and therefore much more dangerous than any enemy, her comrades hit the dirt whenever she picked it up.

Simone paid with her life for her crazed, futile desire to share in the French people's fight, and above all their sufferings, during the German Occupation.

For the rest of his life, André paid for his ill-advised decision to stay in Finland for the sake of mathematics after war was declared. After the Liberation, he naturally considered returning to France to take a university job. The Collège de France was mentioned. Postwar rancor and rivalries, which made it fashionable to try to appear more heroic than one had actually been, resulted in a small cabal of self-righteous professors who toed the line. These managed to block André's return, despite the efforts of several of his colleagues from the Bourbaki group, who defended him fiercely. After André died, a great French mathematician would say that a whole generation of French mathematicians had thus been deprived of one of its greatest masters.

André was not thrilled that he had to spend the rest of his life in Chicago, then Princeton. It had not been his choice. This cozy, but compulsory, exile would affect our family life during my whole childhood and afterwards, for we lived a fragmented life, divided into departures, returns, and above all, long separations.

André did not care much for America per se, despite the excellent work conditions which he found there. He was able to invite many French colleagues to Chicago, and the volumes of Bourbaki's works which appeared at this time list "Nancago" as the place where they were written, since many of the Bourbaki members taught at Nancy, and André was in Chicago. For a time, he hoped that a return to France might be possible. I believe that he made manifold requests, and then, being a pragmatist, he finally gave up. I never heard him complain. But he never became an American citizen, whatever other sources may have claimed.

Near the end of his life, almost by chance, he was reunited with a cousin, the grandson of Hermine's sister, Anna Sternberg. I had arranged the meeting. I drove André to see Otto, who was living near Philadelphia. The two cousins were almost the same age. There was something touching about this reunion of two octogenarians, and naturally they talked about the war. "So, where were you, when did you escape, what route did you take, how did you survive?"

Asking my father if he had become an American citizen, Cousin Otto used an assured tone that implied, "Of course, you took American citizenship?" André looked surprised and replied,

"What for? I am French."

Cousin Otto laughed gently. "That's true, you are French. As for me, I have been Austrian, Czech, Polish, and Belgian. I was never French, but I owe my life to the French."

This is the story of Cousin Otto. It takes place in 1942 in the Pyrenées.

Otto, his wife, and two children were hidden in a barn for several days. Upstairs, under the roof. The farmer brought them food and news reports. After a few more days of waiting, he would be able to get them across the border to Spain.

One night after they have gone to bed, they hear strange noises coming from the main part of the house. Screaming, shouting voices. The farmer must be sloshed. Then everything quiets down again. First thing in the morning, Otto looks outside through a crack between two boards. The farm is located at the top of a hill, offering splendid views. That morning, he sees the farmer lead a dozen policemen, followed by a van, heading straight for the barn.

Otto alerts his wife. The farmer has betrayed them. Which explains his getting sloshed the night before. They hug their children in their arms. The children are old enough to understand, and share their parents' anguish and certainty that, as Otto put it, "we were screwed." Hanging onto one another, they kiss and experience their last moments of freedom. The procession goes around the barn and vanishes, clearly heading for the courtyard, from which they will have access to the barn. From the place where they are cooped up, Otto and his family cannot see the courtyard, but they hear the van's engine. Seconds tick by. Once again the motor roars, and almost immediately Otto, still looking out through the crack in the wall, sees the farmer, policemen, and van reappear and go back down the road in orderly fashion.

Several hours go by. The farm is completely silent. Otto and his wife exhaust themselves in guesswork and wondering what to do next. The children are hungry and thirsty. Finally, the door to their garret opens and a peasant, whom they have never seen before, hands them some food and explains that the night before, the farmer had discovered his wife in bed with another man, and murdered them both. Knocked them out, then stabbed them. Before going to surrender to the police, he went to his neighbor's home to ask him to look after Otto and his family.

Three days later, the neighbor got them across the border into Spain.

Nothing connected Otto to Europe after this. He had become an American, and had never needed a *garde-meuble*.

Jerusalem

THE FIRST TIME THAT ANDRÉ TRAVELED TO ISRAEL, OR MORE precisely Jerusalem, he had a slight stroke. Hysterics and towering rages were among his habitual reactions, but this was more than mere hysterics. It was a genuine blood pressure spike. A real dizzy spell. The hotel doctor had to be called.

It was in September 1979. As a recipient of the Wolf Prize in Mathematics, André was discovering Jerusalem. My mother and I were accompanying him.

Could this blood pressure spike be explained by the fact that he shared the award with Jean Leray, a noted French mathematician who, during the postwar years, distinguished himself by his efforts to prevent André from getting a job in France, "for ethical reasons"?

Had André felt like throwing a fit at the notion of appearing together in Jerusalem with his old enemy, he would have thrown it back in Paris, when he was informed of the award.

It was only the second year of the Wolf Prizes, established by Ricardo Wolf, an elderly German Jew who had emigrated to Cuba before the First World War. A great friend of Fidel Castro, who in 1961 sent him to Tel Aviv as Cuba's ambassador, Wolf was allowed to bring his enormous fortune out with him. Until 1973, Ricardo Wolf retained his status as Cuban ambassador. This was the great era of agricultural cooperation between Cuba and Israel.

I recall that André laughed at the news that he would be going to Jerusalem in the company of Jean Leray. He had observed that the awards seemed to go to teams comprising one Jew and one non-Jew. The year before, the mathematics award went to Carl Ludwig Siegel and Israel Gelfand.

André proclaimed: "I am Leray's Jew!" The very notion put him in a good mood.

Was the blood pressure spike due to the emotion of visiting the Holy Land? Six years before, André had given me a big surprise when the Yom Kippur War broke out. He was at my home in Vermont, where I was teaching, when I received a call from the United Jewish Appeal. They were contacting every Jew they could find to request funds to support Israel. I pledged a modest sum, then hung up and explained to André what it was about.

"Aha, you too."

Looking somewhat sheepish and almost apologetic, he admitted that he had already sent in his own check, adding:

"It's not that I especially love the Jews, or that I think the State of Israel is destined to last very long, given the way it is viewed by its neighbors."

"But?"

"But nothing. I don't especially love the Jews, but I love even less those who want to shove them into the sea."

Did he find it moving to stride through the Holy City's narrow streets, to approach and touch the Western Wall? He was less moved, at first sight, than my mother, who quickly wrote a small note and slid it between two stones. Only the following year, shortly after my marriage to Eric, did she inform me that he was precisely what her note requested. My father, whom my sister had already given a first Jewish son-in-law, did not conceal his satisfaction that I had snagged a second one. Exactly one year after we stood next to it, the *Kotel* (the Wall) had cooperated, and furnished my parents with the Jewish doctor of their dreams.

While my mother's prayer wound its way among the thousands of other prayers carefully rolled and slipped into the cracks between the stones of Herod's Temple, we three paced along the Via Dolorosa, and my father merrily rediscovered a talent for bargaining which he had acquired during his years in India. He bought me a rug which I was longing for. This purchase was not done in a matter of minutes. There were entrances and exits, followed by taking tea with the Arab merchant. Then the merchant and André began repeatedly questioning each other's manhood as well as the other's membership in humanity. "What kind of man are you?" each joyfully demanded in turn. What kind of man to bargain in this manner over a gift for your daughter? What kind of a man to try to sell me this rug at ten times its real value?

I was lost in admiration. I had never seen André like this.

The symptoms of a blood pressure spike, headache and dizziness, occurred one Shabbat, at the end of the day. We had spent the afternoon walking around Jerusalem. The following day, the awards ceremony for the Wolf Prize was to be held at the Knesset. That morning, we were amused to see Jean Leray pacing the hotel lobby, holding a piece of paper in front of his nose, apparently rehearsing his acceptance speech and thank-yous. According to his habit, André merely intended to improvise a few sentences. He much regretted not being able to speak these few sentences in the "lovely Hebrew language," he made a point of saying the next day.

On that fine September Shabbat, my parents and I were walking the streets of Jerusalem when we happened upon an unusual sight, or at least unusual for us. We had reached a hill overlooking one of the city's main roads. The edge of this hill was lined with a small crowd of men, teenagers, and boys, all dressed in black, with black hats and *kippahs*. They gesticulated and spoke loudly, but we only saw them from behind, so at first we did not realize just what they were doing.

We drew nearer. No one deigned to even look at us. All of

them, young and old, big and little, were busy throwing stones onto cars being driven along the road. Obviously, their drivers were violating Shabbat.

I laughingly told André that it seemed a curious way to observe Shabbat with the family, by throwing stones at drivers.

He was not laughing. He took hold of my mother's arm.

"Let's get the hell out of here, these people scare me."

Under his navy blue beret, André looked greenish.

Soon afterward, he complained of a severe headache. We went back to the hotel. My mother and I waited for the doctor. We were worried.

Stretched out on his bed with his eyes shut, André was groaning over and over:

"That Jews could be such idiots! That Jews could be such idiots!"

A Navy Blue Beret

"LET'S GO DRINK SOMETHING AT THE CAFÉ, SHALL WE?" SAYS my father on a sweltering afternoon, so hot that even the chestnut trees in the Luxembourg Gardens have given up providing cool shelter. They are waiting for the evening.

My father offers me his arm, or rather takes mine in his, and we walk haltingly. We are walking, but I have the impression of carrying him. Thus do I carry everything that made me what I am. My father is an old snail, bearer of an old shell which is also, inevitably, my own shell. Despite the heat, the old snail is wearing a dark raincoat and a navy blue beret. My grandparents also moved through the Luxembourg Gardens haltingly, garbed in dark raincoats and berets.

My father's beret is exactly the same as the ones which his father, mother, and sister wore, at the same angle. I have photos of all four, the Weil quartet, taken at different times, happy, unhappy, on vacation, in exile, all together, or just two or three of them, but one constant remains: the Basque beret, which always appears on the head of at least one Weil.

For instance, there is a lovely photo of my grandmother with

Simone at Sitges, Spain, where the latter went to wage war but only succeeded, poor thing, in scalding her leg. In this photo, Simone, still wearing her Anarchist militia uniform and a cap, smiles like an urchin who is having lots of fun. Of all the photos which I possess of her, this is the one in which she seems most openly cheerful. Was it because she had been able to make war a little, even if only for two weeks? Or because she is reunited with her parents again? Sitting, or rather perched, on a low wall, she puts her arm around Mime's shoulders. The latter, leaning against her daughter, seems somewhat tired, but radiantly happy. Just think, she had managed to reclaim her crazy "*trollesse*" in one piece, more or less, in the middle of the Spanish Civil War. Mime is wearing a dark beret, pulled low over her brow.

Whether in Marseilles, New York, or London, Simone always wore a navy blue beret. I imagine that she replaced them from time to time. Where did she get them? My grandmother wore the same kind. Perhaps she bought them in bulk. Mime and Simone also dressed alike, in sweaters hand-knitted by Mime, who knitted endlessly. Later, she would knit for me more dresses than I could ever wear. They were pretty, but dark. Brown, or dark blue. The Weils did not indulge in bright colors.

From January 1930 to May 1932, when he taught in India, my father, who was quite young and something of a dandy, loved to dress up in exotic headgear. Soon after his return to France, he also adopted the beret. I have found a short letter which he sent to his parents in August 1937. On a walking tour of the Savoy region, he writes: "Could you also send me my Basque beret, if Mother knows where it is?"

Therefore I can state with assurance that by age thirty-one, my father was also wearing the family beret.

We sit and order freshly squeezed lemon juice. He speaks to me about a British novel which he is reading. He is all that remains of my family, a concentration of my family. His eyes, or perhaps just his glance, are increasingly like Selma's, nearsighted, doleful, and yet acute, as well as his emphatic way of pronouncing every word.

His slightly lopsided smile is like Simone's in certain photos. His bone structure is my grandfather's. His neck comes from my grandfather. The only difference is that Biri had a scar on his neck, the results of a boil which had to be lanced. My mother used to say that the neck is the most fragile part of a man, what remains of the little boy after he grows up to be an adult. I see my father's neck through my mother's eyes. My father's neck endures pointlessly, since my mother is no longer around to see it.

Some children run by, raising dust. André says:

"Your son's beloved pony surely must have died a long time ago. As I recall, he was named Taquin."

He says this slowly, a little as if he were singing an ancient song. He finishes with a sigh, and a nostalgic "*Eh oui!*"

My son had experienced great difficulties in learning how to walk. Until he was almost four, he always fell and burst out wailing, more from humiliation than pain. André gave him an unlimited allowance for rides on Taquin. He could take as many jaunts as he liked. Impressively seated atop his pony, he forgot all about his tumbles. By age five, he walked more securely, but still loved Taquin. My father offered him a deal. He put coins on the kitchen table, and all those which my son managed to add up correctly, he was allowed to keep. That paid for a good number of rides as well.

We drink our lemon juice, seated on metal chairs. I am safe at home, because my father, even though he is old, frail, and whiny, carries us all in that old shell which is our own. It bears my grandparents, aunt, and mother. And also my son.

Indestructible?

SIMONE, ONE DAY WHEN I LOATHED YOU, I FORGET WHY, AT any rate on that day it was not your fault; sometimes I loathe you foolishly, after speaking too much with one or another of your worshippers of either sex. One of them rebukes me harshly for not being sufficiently enamored of you, yes, enamored, although why should I be enamored of my aunt? Never mind. Another tries to carry me away after her, somewhere in the highest heavens, far from worldly filth, into the empyrean where she floats alongside you, where you have been transformed into a meteor, a shooting star, or who knows what. The French language lacks words radiant and dazzling enough to describe you, and yet my aching eardrums still echo from litanies of words which try to do so, like limpid clarity, or stunning flame.

On such a day when I loathed you, I met a man who had known you in London during the war. And the words used by this man to describe you shattered me. He did not speak of a comet or blinding brightness, but of a tired little young woman, isolated, invisible, dressed like a pauper, wearing a wide beret, retiring, diffident, and silent.

He described you so well, without flowery language but so precisely that suddenly I could see you, sitting in a corner, it seems to have been during a meeting at Oxford, I saw you seated on a chair, quite stooped (your refusal to sit up straight distressed your mother, from the time when she still hoped to marry you off). Your shapeless, overlong skirt swept the floorboards absurdly, as even during wartime, despite everything, young women tried to look pretty. Nobody spoke to you and you remained silent.

I was shattered by this image of you, poor little sister of my father, who called you an "astonishing phenomenon" and a "mushroom in humus soil," the daughter worshipped by my grandparents, their "dear little darling" younger then than my son is today. Lonely and useless in London was the same "Red Virgin" who ten years before had so enjoyed demonstrating with striking workers, defying bosses and bourgeoisie, taunting those in power and making front-page news ("Lady Lycée Teacher Stirs Up Le Puy's Unemployed" reads a January 1932 headline in *La Croix*). Her heart ached with grief because they refused to parachute her into France.

This "*trollesse,*" who was so fragile, wanted to be treated like a man. To be parachuted into France. For God's sake! Was it not enough for her to dip her leg into a potful of boiling oil during the Spanish Civil War? Already, at the time, she had made up her mind to fight, but far from helping her comrades in arms, she made life extremely difficult for them, before finally being rescued by her parents to the great relief of all and sundry. In England, men prepared for parachuting with workout sessions. Did Simone hope for instant death, caused by not knowing how to open the parachute? She was not renowned for her skill with such things. At the very least, she would have broken her legs on impact. And afterwards? Afterwards, she had a whole plan, of course, to be captured (which was inevitable) and tortured by the Germans to allow time for the Resistance fighters parachuting with her to vanish into thin air.

Certainly she had written: *I feel that it is essential and prescribed that I should stand alone, a foreigner and exiled with respect to every human environment, without exception.* But now the poor *trollesse* is letting herself die from despair because no one took her plan seriously. Naturally, those who loved her had no intention of satisfying her thirst for martyrdom. The others simply had no interest in her plan. Perhaps this is what destroyed her, even more than the tuberculosis. Her parents might have been able to save her, once again. But they were far away. They were in New York, pushing my baby carriage in Riverside Park, waiting for Simone's letters from London, filled with heartwarming lies.

This image of Simone as withdrawn, lonely, dismissed, or at least ignored by those whom she so ardently wished to join was new to me, a kind of head-on collision. My father had written that his sister's death took him by surprise, as he always considered her indestructible. Many years after she died, he would persist, continuing to convey this image of Simone to us, his daughters, for in his memory, his female troll of a sister, his "mushroom in humus soil," even though by then long destroyed, remained indestructible.

So the slight young woman dressed like a pauper, wearing a ridiculous beret, spent her days alone in an office, writing reports. She was assigned all this writing to keep her busy, clearly because no one had any idea what to do with her. As for "reports," she wrote her last texts here, which are among her most accomplished and inspired. I am touched by this poor, forsaken "*trollesse*" who, when all is said and done, belongs to my family.

There is a postscript.

You see, this man who met you in London at the end of 1942 also assured me that you were aware of the rounding up and deportation of children, Jewish babies torn from their mothers' arms "under inhuman conditions" (I'm quoting a BBC report from that year), to be shipped to camps at Pithiviers and Drancy. And from Drancy . . . So, if you were informed, why, why, from the depths of your own despair, from which only your parents could have rescued you, as you yourself wrote, why did you not have a thought, a word, for all those Jewish babies, crazed with terror, cruelly separated from their mothers?

Japonaiserie

They were going to conquer the mythical metal
developed by Cipangu in its faraway mines . . .
                                        —José-Maria de Heredia

The Japanese do things thoroughly, so the photo album
is luxuriant. With its cream-colored, imitation-leather cover
decorated with gilded curlicues, it really looks like a wedding
album. The album of my Japanese wedding with my father.

Filling the entire first page of the album is a head-and-shoulders
shot of André, posed rigidly in a tuxedo. He donned the jacket by
itself, since only the upper half of his body was being immortalized. His chest is decorated with the medal which he has just been
awarded, a huge golden thing hanging from his neck on a wide
blue ribbon, like those given to prizewinning livestock at agricultural fairs. The medal is set with large gems, synthetic emeralds,
sapphires, and rubies. Not fake, but synthetic ones, which are entirely different, as the people who bestowed it carefully explained.
These are genuine precious stones, simmered and ripened in the
laboratory, gems to be proud of. I was told, "Your father can be
proud."

In the photo, he does not look proud. Instead, with his lopsided smile, he has the forlorn look of someone who has lost his way.

In an ancient Kyoto neighborhood, a very old father and his daughter walk slowly, along a dark, narrow street lined with low buildings whose windows, if there are any, must look out on the opposite side. They have quietly left the luxury hotel where they are housed, briefly followed a wide avenue, and turned right, heeding instructions from a young receptionist stationed on their floor, instructions given after much faltering, bowing, and giggling behind her hand. The restaurant where she is sending them, all the way on the other side of the river, is unworthy of a famed mathematician invited to Japan to receive the highly prestigious Kyoto Prize.

It is hard to explain to the young woman that they have come from Tokyo a few days early, and their hosts are not yet paying for their meals. Can she grasp that the sensei, the renowned mathematician whose breast will soon be decorated by a superb golden medal, does not have in hand the exorbitant sums needed to dine with his daughter in the hotel restaurants?

The young receptionist is unaware that as soon as he arrived in the luxury hotel's salmon-pink marble lobby, the testy sensei made a terrible scene, bellowing that it was out of the question to stay, even for an hour, in an establishment for nouveau riche businessmen. He only calmed down after his daughter declared that she would find it amusing to stay in a crass, overpriced hotel. A dozen panicked mathematicians and interpreters, draped around telephones in desperate attempts to resolve the crisis, heaved a collective sigh of relief.

It would be useless to explain to the young receptionist that the Weil family traditionally scorns luxury hotels and prefers working-class restaurants.

The street which they are now following, more an alley than a street, is deserted. Apart from the very old father leaning on his daughter's arm.

When I think of the word "leaning," I can feel my father's arm under mine. The comforting warmth of what is familiar. Familiar? When I was young, I never walked arm-in-arm with my father. That role was filled by my mother. But she was buried years ago beneath a Japanese cherry tree, albeit far from Japan. I was obliged to take her place. An ordained, enforced replacement which is highly unpleasant, as my father often tartly points out. Still, that evening, in a dark Kyoto alleyway, the word "leaning" only has good connotations. We are walking slowly. André explains that the red lanterns which add a merry little note here and there, and make me feel like I am walking through a Japanese film set, mean that the house in question is a "Love Hotel." Not really a whorehouse but rather a meeting place, whether for an hour or all night, for couples who are ill-housed in apartments crowded with children and aged parents. My father has long been acquainted with Japan. He explains, I listen, and feel safe. Not displaced, lost in a strange city, a thousand leagues from home, but on the contrary, anchored in a familiar place where I spent part of my childhood, Japan as described by André. Conjoined sea turtles, come from afar and sharing the same old shell, we calmly walk through a dark, slightly mysterious back street in the imaginary land of Japan.

Soon we reach the narrow river, which we cross by bridge. Red paper lanterns mirrored in the inky water announce the restaurant's presence. The humidity rises, wrapping us in a light mist. We are sinking into a film by Mizoguchi, we are at the heart of a dream, in which pretty lanterns softly glow.

In the unpretentious and "cheap" restaurant suggested by the young receptionist, we can barely afford a clear soup in which two shrimp float amid a few cabbage leaves. Helping my father to sit down on the wood floor, I order by pointing to a dish at the next table. Mute and unlettered, I smile, bowing. My smiles and bows irk the noted mathematician. I point out that in a place where no one speaks any language known to us, I have no choice if we want to eat. He admits as much with a shrug of his shoulders. After dinner, he must be lifted, hoisted, and pulled back onto his feet. Several men watch us. It occurs to none of them to offer any help.

A bit later, on the way back in an elderly shuffle, arm-in-arm, it is not a joyful stroll, our conversation is not zestful, but we have eaten, the air seems warmer, and the alleyway cheerier. The Love Hotel lanterns are our friends, landmarks in the all-engulfing mist. Here is the first, second, and finally the third lantern, a bit brighter than the rest. We will soon get there. My father's arm is under mine. Safe and peaceful, André and I are experiencing a Japanese dream.

Suddenly, spontaneously, the word "clutching" appears to replace the word "leaning." My shoulder tenses up in pain, rebelling against the exertion which is being imposed upon it. I feel my father's entire weight bearing down on my arm, the weight of my father's despair. I haul my ancient father along a deserted alleyway, deathly dark and dreary in an imaginary land, in a dream which threatens to become a nightmare.

Japan is an imaginary land, a story that is told to my sister and me. Japanese women wearing kimonos, hiding their mouths behind handheld fans, always photographed against a background of flowering cherry trees, are as mythical to us as the Roman matrons and Greek ladies in our books of tales and legends. The kimono is equivalent to a peplos. During his first long stay in Japan, alone, our father sends us gifts which confirm, by their oddness, our certainty that this land does not exist. Small headless, armless dolls called kokeshi. Tiny boxes covered with unusual fabrics, kimonos whose wide belts leave you breathless, sandals in which it is impossible to stagger more than three steps, and above all, two masks, smooth, white female faces with their lips stretched into bloody red smiles, revealing a splendid row of ink-black teeth.

One day, a character who does seem to exist in flesh and blood makes her entrance in my father's letters. It is a certain Momoko-san, one of the young hostesses employed at a mathematics conference. This appearance does not delight my mother, but we girls immediately accept her. We imagine our father in the company of a young girl whose face is painted white, with a smile that reveals all her teeth, painted black. Perched on our sandals, dressed in our brightly colored kimonos, we are Momoko-san.

When he finally returns, my father has become Japanese. He takes boiling hot baths, then rubs himself with a long, narrow towel like a scarf, thin as a handkerchief. He manages to temporarily convince us to give up our large terry towels, so comfy and reassuring. He forces us to eat with chopsticks. One day he even tries to teach us to bow. His lessons are excellent, but we laugh so much that our own bows are quite spoiled. He informs us that when they answer the phone, the Japanese do not say "Hello," but instead shout out as quickly as possible: "*Mushi mashi!*" Delighted by the strange syllables, we chant them at the top of our lungs. When the telephone rings, we dash for it and whoever grabs the receiver first gets to yell: "*Mush'mashi! Mush'mashi!*" On the other end of the line, my father's friends and colleagues, all of them sensible adults, are surprised. They make fun of us, finding us bad-mannered. We do not care. We make bows, we eat with chopsticks, we call ourselves Momoko-san, and we are Japanese women, denizens of an imaginary land.

And on one warm, gray autumn afternoon, my father and I landed in Tokyo, in the land of the white masks with black teeth, the imaginary land. Many years have passed, and now we are a very old father and a daughter who looks nothing like a little girl.

Who looks nothing like a little girl, but who is nonetheless lost in wonderment, while realizing that it is absurd, that we are walking normally, not upside down, that our luggage has not changed shape or grown lighter, and that the car we climb into is in every way similar to the one which dropped us off at the airport the day before. The cloudy sky, scrawny trees lining the expressway, and traffic jams are in no way exotic.

My father's voice is also the same, bossy and impatient: "Give me your hand, I cannot see anything. With my poor eyesight, how am I expected . . ."

Was I convinced that once in Japan, André Weil, almost as world-famous for his impatience as for his mathematical genius, would suddenly become patient? That he would complain less? Had I believed that his vision would improve?

At the hotel, a boardinghouse for intellectuals in Tokyo's university quarter, where, we are informed, a special air conditioner blasts out air which is highly stimulating for brain activity, a small reception has been waiting for hours. A very old mathematician, a longtime friend of my father's, several still-young professors, and a few students. The latter are naturally moved and honored to welcome the famed professor, the venerable sensei who has come to Japan to receive the nation's most exalted award. In any case, they had no choice. Everyone, young and old, mobilized for this first welcoming, is loaded down with gifts.

I offer thanks and smiles. I would like my expressions of gratitude to be appropriate. I would like to display a courtesy which matches that of our hosts. I would like to be as gracious as the young women who smilingly offer me pretty packages. I start bowing my head, the head of a European woman eager to show her good intentions. Then, bit by bit, I get carried away. The bows are contagious. In spite of myself, I attempt proto-bows, embryonic bows. I realize I am stiff, clumsy, and surely absurd.

Added to my desire to master bowing is a sudden regret that my hair is not straight. With my frizzy mop of hair, I feel somehow unkempt.

I would like my father to understand my wishes, and cooperate with me to offer the people who welcome us a presentation as smooth and polished as their own.

Japan is a country where feelings are hidden, he told us after his first stay, during which he became Japanese. They say: "I missed our appointment last night because my mother died." These words are accompanied by a smile, or better yet, a flustered giggle.

My father skillfully imitated the voice, expression, half-bow, and above all, the flustered giggle. He explained that the point is to not make the other person feel uncomfortable, to not impose one's own grief upon him. So, my mother is dead and then a little giggle. Sorry to have possibly made you uncomfortable.

Fascinated, we began to picture it. We pictured the country where sadness is hidden beneath laughter, even of the flustered kind.

Now that we are here in Japan, I would have liked my father to become Japanese once again. That he recall the dead mother and flustered laughter. But it has been ages since André played along. He is old; he no longer wishes to be Japanese. He does not give a hint of even a trace of a bow. A hint would suffice, given his advanced age. But no, he hints nothing whatsoever. He does not feel the slightest desire to be courteous or gracious. He could not care less if others feel comfortable or not. He declares that the hotel is horrible, and that the pile of gifts will burden us unduly.

I wish I could force him to be polite. I am ashamed of my father, who refuses to be Japanese. I feel responsible. A lady who is no longer young, wearing a dark kimono, tells me smilingly between two deep bows, as if she were offering a compliment: "This stay will be very tiring for you." I bow. I return her smile. I think I have just discovered the bow of solidarity, surely a woman thing.

It requires thirty years of apprenticeship to become a master Bunraku puppeteer. Ten years to learn how to move the feet, ten years for the left hand, and ten years for the head and right hand.

As for me, I had to improvise. The puppet whose proper functioning I am responsible for during this trip is not a young girl unhappily in love, with a delicate neck, frail fingers emerging from the wide sleeves of a splendid kimono, whose minute gestures draw tears from the most jaded audiences, nor is it a brave and handsome samurai warrior, who carefully prepares his own suicide, supported with loving concern by three puppeteers, and accompanied by musicians' heart-rending songs and the audience's sobbing.

My puppet is an old professor invited to Japan to receive a prize which is being offered too late, since his mate is buried beneath a cherry tree, and now he is alone, sad, and old.

This puppet's head remains upright by itself. But his face is far from presenting the hoped-for expression. I would wish for him to have the serene expression of an old sage, full of kindness and forbearance.

The serene old sage full of kindness is a different puppet. Not the one I have been given. All too often for my liking, mine displays an exasperated, impatient, miserable, and despairing face.

With all my energy, I pull on the strings for a smile. I struggle against the despair of my puppet.

My puppet scoffs at my exertions. Moreover, it is far from defenseless, and misses no opportunity to put me down and remind me who is playing the main part here. For instance, by telling me: "Let me point out that your own talents would never get you such an invitation as this."

It also keeps some wonderful surprises up its sleeve, transforming itself when required into a fine, brilliant professor, perfectly mastering his subject, it goes without saying, as well as his voice, glances, and smallest gestures.

His hands are youthful and vivacious, his fingers slightly separated, his glance is nearsighted but acute, his face is luminously austere, his voice is confident, with precise, well-constructed sentences reeled off in a slightly ironic tone.

I feel like I am fourteen years old again. With eyes and ears wide open, I look and listen with such pride, while my father, the famed mathematician, holds forth in front of an auditorium full of people who feverishly write down his every word.

When I was fourteen, such moments lasted forever, and my role was that of a dazzled spectator. I had no idea that one day I would become a puppeteer. Now I tremble in fear that my puppet might suddenly collapse, flaccid and spineless, beneath the flawless tweed suit which I had him put on earlier. I am mistaken. It does not collapse. For several hours, my father forgets that he is, and hates being, old.

Ages ago, André, imbued with literary classics, admirably performed old fogey roles to entertain his wife and two daughters. But this character of a tetchy elder, so delightful in Molière's comedies and Plautus's farces, has no place in the performance to which we have been invited. I was not given the responsibility of transporting a doddering comedy puppet to Japan, freshly garbed and performance-ready, but an eminent professor puppet.

I take this assignment seriously, for it is an immense and splendid performance, staged in the land of masks and smiles which hide feelings which should be hidden.

I take my assignment all the more seriously because, playing opposite us, in a silent dialogue (since we hardly exchange a word), a giant of Japanese film and his daughter reflect an image of what we ought to be like. The other father will also receive a golden medal set with rubies and emeralds. This father and daughter look alike, just as my father and I look alike. About a head taller than us, they are smooth, where we are crumpled. Upright and imposing, statue-like, they flow easily while we stumble. The daughter's haughty, inscrutable smile, appearing above a hot pink suit, seeks, derides, and crushes me. It rubs me out.

So I pull on my puppet's strings, the strings of the smile which conceals feelings. I allow myself no breather, for the show is continuous, with rare intermissions. Seated at the table, my father is fumbling, hunched over his plate. Leaning towards him, I guide his blind chopsticks while urging him in an undertone to be polite to our samurai-masked hosts. In French, André complains to me that there is nothing to eat, and asks if this damned meal will ever end, and I translate into English: "My father is delighted, and thinks the dinner is delicious."

When our hosts push him against his will into a wheelchair, for they correctly fear that he walks too slowly for a palace visit to be completed on schedule, I run alongside the wheelchair, which a young man wearing a laughing mask pushes at a spanking pace. The wheels squeak on the gravel. Around us, everyone is running, laughing, and taking photos. These photos will appear in newspapers, albums, and books. I will later realize that it hardly matters that, from the depths of his wheelchair, the sensei from afar is declaring furiously that the tour is pointless, the palace is revoltingly newfangled and crass. All that matters is that the tour occurred. But I am not yet aware of this. Breathless, straining my neck and back to lean over him while running, permanently smiling like a thrilled tourist for the cameras, I fiercely whisper in his ear: "Smile anyway, just pretend."

He suddenly smiles maliciously, informing me that my automatic laugh goes well with the Japanese ones. As for me, I would so much prefer it if he wore the fierce expression of the Nara Temple's tutelary gods, with their huge eyebrows bulging with rage, and mouths spewing maledictions. Or even the features, convulsed with fear, of a famous Kabuki actor playing an equally famous huntsman who goes insane at the foot of Mount Fuji. Even if my father is not a huntsman gone insane at the foot of Mount Fuji, nor a Nara Temple tutelary god, other appropriately Japanese models do exist, since he rejects the smile which hides feelings.

The awards ceremony is a grand performance, complicated and fine-tuned, like clockwork. An apparently endless cast of characters fills the stage: ambassadors, interpreters, little kimono-clad girls waiting for their cue to start singing and then offer the three prizewinners decorative balls embroidered with multicolored thread. There are also several rows of Japanese notables whose role is to sleep like logs while seated rigidly with their necks perfectly upright.

The tuxedoed sleepers lined up in their chairs are large puppets who require no exertion from anyone. They do not speak, nor do they sing, and only require to be seated, after which they fall asleep without even tilting their heads. Conspicuously placed in front of the rows of notables are two splendid and graceful puppets, tall and slender. Seated on white armchairs, they are two Imperial Highnesses, a prince and his wife, fairy tale characters, eternally young and lovely, elegant and smiling.

Every possible empty space onstage is occupied by a female character dressed in a gorgeously hued kimono. I gather that the stage director wanted to scatter bright, joyous tones amid the crowd of black tuxedos.

During the ceremony, I had to entrust my old puppet to others. I sit in the auditorium, banished to the audience. Others will lead the old mathematical giant onto the stage. They will position him on a chair between the two other giants, the great master of Japanese film and an American scientist. My father is a short, scrawny giant whose disoriented look inspires pity. Later, he will need to be guided when it is his turn to receive the award.

The two other prizewinners are flawless. The Japanese man, tall and broad-shouldered, wearing an inscrutable mask, masters the art of bowing with strict, highborn pride. The decidedly huge American, hulking and paunchy, wears the ruddily pink, solemn mask of a man convinced that the award which he will receive is fully deserved.

My father is the one whose upper face is devoured by huge sunglasses, which they dug up somewhere backstage, for he is driven mad by the harsh lighting required by the photographers capturing the event. Even devoured by sunglasses, his face looks exposed, his mouth twisted by stress and exhaustion. The face of a flayed man, a torture victim instead of a prizewinner.

It seems to me that in this land of masks, someone might have found a mask for him, no matter which one, since the choices abounded: the mask of a happily smiling prizewinner, an inscrutably smiling mask, an arrogantly brutal samurai mask, or a Noh theater old man's mask with a long white silky beard, with deeply etched features marked by patrician grief. The *Koushi-jyo* mask, a ghost disguised as a wrinkled old man with bleak eyes and sorrowful mouth whose edges turn downward towards a horsehair goatee, would have suited the occasion admirably, as well as my father's frail figure.

Or if nothing else, a bright red or gilded devil's mask, with scary eyes, horns, and sneering mouth. Anything but the obscenity of allowing my father to be the only one to advance onstage with his face exposed.

Just when he receives his award, the old and eminent mathematician from afar leans forward slightly, with the resignation of someone bowing before fate, his face devoured by sunglasses. The face of a flayed man.

This photo causes me pain.

I think it is time to reveal the name of the Japanese film giant, a giant in every sense of the word. It was none other than Akira Kurosawa. My father and he found themselves face-to-face during a reception. André was sincerely pleased to meet the creator of *Rashomon* and *Seven Samurai*. Kurosawa leaned toward my father. The latter, raising his head, said with a modest, yet conniving, grin (after all, it was a conversation between giants, and photographers aptly trained their cameras on them):

"I have a great advantage over you. I can love and admire your work, but you cannot love or admire my work."

Some saw this as a backhanded compliment, which was far from André's intent.

Once the various events and ceremonies were done, the three recipients of the Kyoto Prize were brought to Tokyo to be introduced to the Emperor. On a splendid autumn morning, we gathered in a hotel lobby to wait for the taxis which would bring us to the Imperial Palace. André was bored and found the silence oppressive. He was seated on a couch next to Kurosawa. He turned to him and asked:

"Does the Emperor like your films?"

There was a brief silence. Then came the response:

"His Majesty is a great Emperor."

And the giant of Japanese film bowed slightly, as if to add solemnity to his reply.

Naturally, the palace visit had to follow strict protocol. The three prizewinners would be escorted into a large and beautiful room, in which three little cabins, like voting booths, had been set up. The prizewinners were each asked to enter a little cabin and wait there. Then, the Emperor and Empress would sit for a moment opposite each prizewinner, offering a few congratulatory words. Only the American giant's wife would remain with her husband in his voting booth. After Kurosawa's daughter and I accompanied our eminent fathers up to the doorway of the large room, we would be shut up in an antechamber.

One hour later, in front of the Imperial Palace, a crowd of reporters waited for the three recipients of the Kyoto Prize to emerge. Camera lenses clicked and questions erupted.

The next day, the official report was published: "The friendly manner of the Emperor and Empress left a deep impression on the laureates, providing them with an unforgettable experience."

On the last page of the album are the three prizewinners. They pose in tuxedos, their chests decorated by large gold medals hanging from their necks. Their hands are all intertwined in front of them, which is to say in front of the wrinkled old dwarf situated between two giants glowing with health and vigor, the giant of Japanese film who puckers his lips into a barely amused, somehow scornful pout, and the portly pink American scientist who wears a wide, happy smile. Jammed between these two, the old dwarf, my father, is having a really good laugh. He has managed to yank his left hand away from the pile of hands in front of him. A strong and lively hand, with fingers slightly apart. He never did need a mask. He is free.

Pulling the Wool
over Her Eyes

WITHIN THE FAMILY, WE ALL SPOKE ABOUT SIMONE'S ART-
lessness. It was a recurring subject of conversation.

"Poor Simone, they pulled the wool over her eyes."

How many times, when I was little, and not so little, did I hear
my mother, as well as Simone's cousins, tell how Selma would
serve her daughter the highest-quality cut of beef, while assuring
her that it was the worst cut, claiming that she had bought from
the butcher exactly what the wives of working men, or even the
unemployed, had purchased. Or how she was served flawless pears
purchased in a gourmet shop (Simone refused to eat even slightly
damaged fruit, finding it disgusting) while claiming, without bat-
ting an eyelid, that the pears were practically given away that very
morning at the market.

In order to persuade her daughter, who held a degree in philosophy but was obsessed with the desire to live like the most unfortunate, she claimed to have stood in line with impoverished-looking
housewives, and to have seen them buying the same grapes and
asparagus. She almost went as far as claiming to have found them
in garbage bins. Sheer fairy tales.

In the family, they repeatedly commented how "Selma made her daughter believe that filet mignon was cat food."

One and all would exclaim: "And Simone never suspected a thing!"

Of course, the subject was never discussed in front of my grandparents.

When I was around eleven or twelve, I started to receive an allowance. I saved it, and as soon as it added up to a banknote, I would hide it in a book. The family exclaimed with surprise, "She is doing the same thing Simone did!" I was immediately informed that my banknotes would not grow back. This is how I learned that Simone always stored her money in a book. As she gradually spent it, by sending contributions to unemployment funds all over France, her mother would surreptitiously replace the banknotes. When she was not present, she would instruct someone else to do so.

Later, after I became a mother, I told myself that Mime and Biri wanted their daughter, their "unreasonable *trollesse,*" to quote my grandmother, to eat properly from time to time. Who could blame them?

My mother loved to tell, with a note of comic resentment, but resentment nonetheless, that on one occasion Simone, who was away from Paris, asked her parents to shelter a man just out of prison (the story did not explain why he had been convicted), and my grandparents settled him into the studio of my parents, who were on vacation. Charity is all well and good, said my mother, but why put this man in my room, instead of Simone's?

When they returned, my parents found that their guest had absconded with a number of their belongings in his suitcase. Many years later, my mother still spoke about how Simone's protégé had even stolen her slippers, lovely ones which were a gift from my father.

My mother ended with an ironic wince: "A nice gift for his girlfriend." To which she added that when she complained to my grandmother, the latter replied:

"I will replace whatever he stole from you, but above all, not a word to Simone; it would cause her too much pain."

The family noted, "A fine example of the way in which she was deceived."

My father always defended his sister in discussions, but conceded that she misjudged people, and could not see them the way they really were.

I was not convinced that it would have caused Simone any pain. Surely she would have assumed that a fellow just out of prison had the right to pilfer a few shirts, and even a pair of slippers. Simone never recognized people the way they were, and even less did she think about slippers.

All during my teen years, I swung back and forth like a pendulum between the commonsense viewpoint, of daily life as it is—a daily life which I liked—and the viewpoint of Simone, who charged ahead, following her own plan, without wasting any time on thinking about slippers, or looking at people, meat, or vegetables very closely.

Sometimes, just because life itself interested me, I joined those who felt that Simone might have benefited from learning a little about the reality of things, and that her parents were wrong to wrap her in a cocoon of lies. Sometimes, as a teenager dreaming of heroism and noble adventure, and rebelling against hideous, contemptible petit bourgeois common sense as exemplified by my mother and my cousins, I would fly to the side of Simone, who belonged to a wholly different species.

Would Simone have been different, had the wool never been pulled over her eyes?

Tzedakah

ONE NIGHT DURING A NEW YORK SNOWSTORM, AS I WAS
going home after teaching my classes, a beggar approached me
on Broadway. When it snows heavily at night, the lights on the
avenue play odd tricks, and anyone emerging from the darkness
looks ghostly. So a huge ghost suddenly stood before me, wrapped
in a grayish, filthy blanket, a ghost with a white-haloed black face,
for his dreadlocked hair was covered with a thick layer of snow.

He called out to me in a rather unfriendly way, something on
the order of: "Hey lady, when you can afford a mink coat, you
don't refuse a coin to a poor guy who sleeps outside."

I replied that of course I would give him something, but insisted
on explaining that my fake fur coat was purchased at a flea market.
He looked amazed.

"Oh yeah? That's not a real mink?"

"No, I am not the kind of person who would wear a mink coat.
Not my style, nor my budget."

"But is it as warm as a mink?"

I laughed.

"I have no idea, because I have never worn one, but I doubt it. The wind goes right through it. I imagine that this doesn't happen with a real fur coat. And then the hair is a little sticky, so the snowflakes cling to it, and it becomes quite heavy."

Just then, I said to myself, "Sylvie, do you realize that you are discussing the quality of your coat with a man who sleeps in the street, wrapped in an old blanket?"

Yet he seemed sincerely interested.

"Anyway, this coat is an amazingly good copy. I really believed it was mink."

"If you look closely, you can see right away that it is not. Pure acrylic."

I had opened my handbag, and while speaking, I took out my change purse. My ghost stopped me with a gesture.

"The conversation is enough. Thanks."

I insisted a little, but he shook his head, and vanished in the white-tinted darkness. I saw him again once or twice, after which he must have changed neighborhoods.

I tell this story because it is one I enjoy, but I have no intention of weighing it down with meaning, although it is connected to what follows.

The reader will have noticed that there is much mention made of charity in the descriptions of Simone's ancestors. Her great-great-grandmother Mrs. Barasch was so renowned for her benevolence that even a wicked bandit had heard of it.

So when Simone, as a young teacher at Le Puy, placed her wages on the counter of a café patronized by the unemployed, so that they could help themselves at will—an image of my aunt which delighted me during my high-school days—perhaps she was only following in her own way the precedent of our ancestors, devoted to *tzedakah*.

Tzedakah is a theme in every tale, novel, travel account, or correspondence describing the lives of Jews in every place and time.

Tzedakah translates as "charity," but *ba'al tzedek* signifies a master of justice. The term is identical. Charity is a form of justice, a way of restoring balance.

Simone writes, *The Gospel makes no distinction between the love of our neighbor and justice.* She immediately adds: *In the eyes of the Greeks also, a respect for Zeus the suppliant was the first duty of justice.**

And yet the authors of the Gospel, if not all Jews, were at the very least immersed in Jewish society. Which Simone typically (given her markedly steadfast denial of any continuity between Judaism and Christianity) chooses to overlook.

Here I am broaching a truly complex topic. I am neither a Talmudist nor a philosopher, and even less a saint, yet since I am discussing my aunt, I cannot avoid briefly addressing the subject of charity, about which she was obsessed.

The tales of Central European Jewry swarm with splendid instances of *tzedakah*. A certain rabbi sneaks into a forest by night, unbeknownst to anyone, to gather firewood for a poor widow. A certain rich old miser, loathed by the whole town for his stinginess, throws out any poor beggars who visit him, after asking how much they need. Naturally, after the miser dies, it is revealed that every Friday before dawn, he would drop off an envelope in front of each poor man's door with the exact sum required. A certain rich man hosts a Shabbat dinner for the district's poor people, and when his wife suggests that they eat in the kitchen, explains that one does not send God to eat in the kitchen . . .

I deeply regret that Simone never read these tales, and that her fervent interest in folktales from around the world excluded only those which had beguiled her ancestors' ears and imaginations.

These ancestors always took seriously the commandment in Deuteronomy: "Thou shalt not harden thy heart, nor shut thy hand from thy brother in need."

---

*Translator's note: Simone Weil, *Waiting for God,* trans. Emma Craufurd (New York: G. P. Putnam's Sons, 1951), 139.

For the idea of charity is at the heart of Judaism. The duty of compassion towards one's neighbor is all-important. It is better to give cheerfully, or even better, in secret, but in any case one must open one's hand. What about misers? Very simple! You call on them and you force them to give.

The Talmud establishes a whole system of mandatory, universal community chests, soup kitchens, and cash allotments. It describes in great detail every case in which it is required to be "open-handed" and give to the poor man "according to his needs."

If a poor man lacks the money to buy cookware, he must be given cookware. If the poor man is lonely, a wife must be found for him.

For a poor man who was once rich and previously carried out his business on horseback, a saddle horse must be obtained.

All this gave rise to highly diverting discussions among rabbis. A small example is whether it is worse to walk around naked or hungry. Rav Huna states that if a naked beggar appears, he should be given clothes urgently, without any inquiries to prove that he is as poor as he claims to be. By contrast, Rav Yehuda states that no inquiry is needed when a poor man asks for food, but if he is naked, an inquiry must be made to "see" if he is really naked!

This is what my ancestor Mr. Barasch read about, when he dipped into the Talmud. Perhaps from time to time, lulled by the voices rising from the shop below, where his worthy wife handed out clothing and candy to poor children, perhaps he closed his eyes to imagine rabbis in discussion, seated in an inner courtyard, moistening their lips with large wine cups, under the starry Babylonian sky. No, that would be more like *The Thousand and One Nights*. Grandfather Barasch was well aware that many Talmudic sages, including some of the most eminent, were poor men, choosing to follow humble trades like porter or salt-bearer, earning just enough to feed their families, and devoting themselves body and soul to the study of the Torah. Even more highly respectable ancestors for Simone.

Simone steered clear of the Talmud, and I suspect that she

would have only despised such debates as persnickety and pedestrian.

As a young teacher, she often left money on her desk so that people poorer than her might help themselves. Later, her thinking would go beyond social reality, to develop into mystical meditation.

Yet the beautiful pages which she wrote during the last years of her life about loving one's neighbor have a Talmudic aspect. Like the rabbis, she studies various cases, twirling them in every direction, and also like the rabbis, she embeds the idea of charity within a mystical program which goes beyond mere alms-giving.

The Talmudic sages imagine a man who brings a gift to the King. It is uncertain whether the King's servants will agree to accept and pass along this gift. But the Holy One, Blessed is He, is entirely different from the King. He who gives a coin to the poor man shall deserve and receive the Shekhinah, the Divine Presence.

What is important to the rabbis, above all, is to make the mystical experience not seem out of reach.

Simone, on the other hand, reserves the mystical experience for the happy few. *He who gives bread to the famished sufferer for the love of God will not be thanked by Christ. He has already had his reward in this thought itself.**

But Simone is not just a mystic; she is also a philosopher who knows how to wield paradoxes warily: *It is not surprising that a man who has bread should give a piece to someone who is starving. What is surprising is that he should be capable of doing so with so different a gesture from that with which we buy an object.*†

Jewish charity is in no way paradoxical. The beggar represents God. By giving to the beggar, you are giving to God.

Obviously, the philosopher can be more exacting than rabbis, since she does not lead a congregation. She is not responsible for a community's life and activity, or making sure that funds are di-

*Translator's note: Simone Weil, *Waiting for God*, 151.
†Translator's note: Ibid., 147.

vided more or less justly. Even if two or three times she did enjoy forcing "misers" to spit out donations, I cannot imagine Simone, who so lacked common sense that her mother expressed concern several times in letters to my grandfather, organizing clothing drives for the naked, or meals for the hungry.

Loving thy neighbor is the subject of her meditation, and for this meditation, she creates a landscape which is closer to the Gospels than to 1930s France:

Christ taught us that the supernatural love of our neighbor is the exchange of compassion and gratitude which happens in a flash between two beings, one possessing and the other deprived of human personality. One of the two is only a little piece of flesh, naked, inert, and bleeding beside a ditch; he is nameless . . . Those who pass by this thing scarcely notice it, and a few minutes afterward do not even know that they saw it.* As we know, the one who stops is the much talked about Samaritan.

Everyone loves the Good Samaritan. As children, we learned to follow his example. Simone too loved, but did not identify with, the Good Samaritan, or with him alone. In the conversation between the Samaritan and the poor man being helped, she is both of them, with a preference for the poor man. Her whole energy is focused in this direction, to be the poor man, the hungry, oppressed, enslaved, and suffering man.

Those who lived with Simone were well aware that when a Good Samaritan would stop to help her, she would send him packing, commanding him to go help someone more unfortunate than herself.

When the rabbi gathered firewood for the widow, his purpose was not to acquire blisters or backaches. He did it so that the widow could heat her home, and of course, to be closer to God.

But Simone is something else! When working on a farm, she gathers big armfuls of thistles with her bare hands. Perhaps she hopes to be useful. I am not sure. She is mainly motivated by a

---

*Translator's note: Simone Weil, *Waiting for God*, 146.

fierce desire to feel the pain of farmworkers, even after she is informed that the latter (men who are sturdier than she) wear gloves and use pitchforks. They will soon realize that there is no point in arguing, that Simone is determined to scrape her hands. That evening she will barely eat anything, and sleep on the ground.

Simone's true plan is to feel the pain of poor people, not to provide them with bread or clothing. Her personal brand of charity is to become the beggar and then refuse any help. As she admitted, she commits the sin of envy when she thinks of Christ on the cross.

My insufferable aunt, my saintly aunt, that amazing one-woman outfit perpetually grinding out publicity for poverty, misery, and misfortune!

Now the pendulum has swung in the opposite direction. I find myself on the other side, that of common sense and sound judgment, of the calm and peaceful charity of my modest grandmothers, who handed out clothing and meals, of the Good Samaritan whom I imagine as well-fed and not loathing comfort. Or even on André's side, my father who never aspired to sainthood, but who never in all his life refused money to anyone who asked, and without taking any pride in it, helped his friends' widows, penniless youngsters, and many others.

Obviously, the beauty of Simone's meditation is that it situates itself in an entirely different reality.

He who treats as equals those who are far below him in strength really makes them a gift of the quality of human beings, of which fate had deprived them. As far as it is possible for a creature, he reproduces the original generosity of the Creator with regard to them. *

A reality which leaves far behind the world as it is.

Quite recently, I was in a New York subway car, seated next to a homeless man, not dressed in rags but with a famished look in his eyes, who spent a good fifteen minutes explaining to everyone within earshot how he planned to spend the small sum which

*Translator's note: Simone Weil, *Waiting for God,* 144.

he had just received. He was going to get laid. He chanted: "No money, no honey, no pussy." Paying no attention to the inflexibly blank expressions and resolutely lowered eyes of the people facing him, he favored us with a description which was poetic by dint of its obscenity, a kind of epic poem whose two heroes were "my balls," about the pleasures he was anticipating.

I thought about what I was writing, and therefore about my aunt. I asked myself if she would have disgustedly moved away. Maybe not. She was not, or claimed not to be, prudish. Her biographers never tire of telling how she wanted to accompany her male buddies to a brothel, dressed as a boy. Prostitution fascinated and appalled her. During the war, when a Marseilles policeman threatened to throw her in jail among the prostitutes, she replied that she had always wanted to learn about that milieu.

For Simone, would this man whose balls had invaded the subway car as sole official and glorious representatives of his person, and whose speech—fairly amusing, I must admit—drowned out his obvious despair, deserve the rank of *little piece of flesh, naked, inert, and bleeding beside a ditch*?

The Old Horse

"YOU MUST FEEL LIKE YOU ARE WALKING AN OLD, BLIND, AND deaf dog who cannot take three steps without stopping."

"I do not own a dog. Besides, you're not an old dog, you're an old horse. An old horse who knows the route."

"I have forgotten all the routes."

I try to make light of things.

"You were accustomed to always dash around, now you no longer dash. Everything is relative."

My father, an old man who is now slightly shorter than me, walks alongside me, leaning on his cane. A cane which I have glued together and patched up a dozen times, since he is attached to it and does not want a replacement.

He continues:

"All the same, it must be boring for you to have to walk so slowly."

"Do I have a choice?"

"No."

He looks up at me sadly, but somewhat ironically too, and sighs loudly.

"My poor daughter!"

Then he declaims:

"*O che sciagura d'essere senza coglioni!** It would be better for you if I died."

When the conversation reaches this point, I am pitiless.

"Could be, but I can't bludgeon you to death. It's not done. Even if you were a dog, I could not do it."

"It must have been done in some cultures. It might still occur. Bludgeoning old parents. That would simplify things."

I laugh.

"Bludgeon them and then maybe eat them?"

The soft click of the cane on the road. We are going to have lunch at the Institute in Princeton. The New Jersey autumn is strikingly ablaze this year. I collect dead leaves colored red and yellow and show them to my father, who reminds me that he can no longer see anything.

"Speaking of eating family members, did you ever suspect at the time that we ate your Frango?"

Frango was my pet chicken in Brazil, which I led around everywhere by a ribbon around its neck.

"I guessed as much. Soon after we left Brazil. I cannot remember how I knew. By age six, I realized that my parents were traitors and cannibals."

He laughs in turn.

"Some God, I am not sure which, punished us and avenged Frango. We were terribly sick all night long. Do you remember much of Brazil?"

"The hot air balloons on the Festa Junina."

"Ah yes, that was pretty. And you must remember our walks up to the radio tower. How you loved to play at being lost."

---

*Translator's note: "Oh, what a misfortune to be a eunuch!" This Italian expression appears in Voltaire's *Candide*, spoken by a eunuch confronted by a naked woman.

We walk for a moment in silence. Then, raising his head, he declares:

"I have had a good life. I have nothing to complain about. Except that your mother died too soon. Apart from that, I have had a good life."

André is not one to say passed away, passed on, or departed. He says "died."

He turns his head towards me and adds:

"You too, you have had a good life."

Suddenly I am filled with anger, and bitterness. The look I have just given him cannot have been friendly. Only an unabashed egoist would label my existence a "good life." I realize that he is thinking of his sister, hooked on misfortune even unto death, whereas he saw her as indestructible. Naturally, he is not thinking of my own more commonplace afflictions, including a son who is just handicapped enough not to have what might be called a "good life" of his own, and a stillborn baby.

Yet immediately, the blindingly brilliant fact becomes obvious: we were not deported to Auschwitz, I was not hidden in a cupboard, I did not witness my parents being tortured, and they did not see their infant thrown to the dogs. I was never forced to work in a factory, and a professor's life is, after all, relatively easy. So obediently and compliantly, the label "good life" affixes itself to the volume—which I still see as a clumsily packaged item—entitled *Life of Sylvie Weil*.

Of course, I do not tell him all that. I just remind him of a sentence by Solon which he had quoted to me the day before, "Call no man happy until he is dead."

He nods his head.

"That is true."

We walk for a moment in silence. He suddenly stops in front of a brilliant red maple tree and faces me. He tells me that a famous physicist, whose name I have forgotten, halted like this during a stroll with his wife, approached her, and put his hands on her shoulders. She thought he was going to kiss her. He dropped dead at her feet.

"I would have liked to die that way too."

A few days later, when we were again walking to the Institute cafeteria where he liked to eat lunch, I recalled our conversation about the "good life." It seemed to me that along the same lines, the time had come to thank André for having left some property to his daughters, like a good middle-class father. He shrugged his shoulders.

"I could not care less what happens after I die."

"Maybe. But I wanted to thank you. Which I just did."

We walked up to the cafeteria, took our trays, and sat down by ourselves at a large table. Just when he was going to dig in, he, who never spoke of such things, put down his knife and fork, raised his head to look at me, and said very slowly, as if he were searching for the words: "Money can also sometimes help to avoid Auschwitz."

Visitation Rights

Now it will be my turn to visit the four Weils in jail. At least they are together in the same cell, Mime and Biri, Simone and André. It is a maximum security prison, which is a good thing in a certain way, since it is for the protection of the prisoners, so that no one attacks or kidnaps them. Still, the system is not quite perfected, because even though you are frisked at the entrance to make sure you are not carrying weapons or bombs, on the way out no one even looks in your handbag. No doubt this explains the harsh monitoring of any contacts you might have during the visit with the beloved prisoner, or prisoners.

For her entire life, my aunt wanted to experience being inside a prison. Now she has her wish. As for her parents and brother, they are locked up because of her.

The last time I went to see them, I was berated by a brutal female prison guard. She decided that my leaving a shoulder bag under a table at the entryway was not enough, and my handbag, which held my change purse, eyeglasses, and handkerchief, was inappropriate for the visiting room where various family members would be brought so that I could spend some time with them.

I told myself that rules are to be expected. I do not want other people kidnapping my family members, and this person is officially responsible for the safety of my close relatives who must remain present and presentable. Even so, I tried to explain that I had the right to family visits, of which this was one, that I had always taken the greatest care of my family, and having signed, years ago, the papers which committed them to the highly honorable institution which took charge of them, I was not now going to roll them into a ball and stuff them into my handbag, this Weil family who wrote on onionskin paper which is entirely suitable for rolling into a ball. When I signed the *lettre de cachet,* I did not know that the honorable institution would henceforth treat me like a criminal, each time I came to offer some comfort to my little Weils by speaking silently to them in a familiar idiom.

That morning, I wrote my name in the visitors' book, but did not sign on the dotted line, which led to more squawking.

I had no time to inform the fanatical official that some objects and letters were, like myself, only visiting, and were entitled to return home with me if they pleased, or if I were inclined to take them back. Nor to explain to her that it was already hard enough to make prison visits to letters which discuss me, as well as all kinds of objects which filled my childhood and youth, without getting screamed at on top of everything.

The affable harridan threatened to call her supervisor. Finally she did not do so, which disappointed me, as I would have liked to meet the director of the institution where several members of my family are put up for an indefinite time.

They are brought to me in different-sized boxes made of wood and cardboard. Misty-eyed, I pick up one or two of the letters which I skimmed through as a kid, crouched in front of the manuscripts cupboard, or which I carefully brought to read in bed, at the rue Auguste-Comte apartment, early in the morning, when the rising sun stained crimson the wall pockmarked by bullets during the Liberation of Paris. Now these letters bear numbers written in pencil by an unfamiliar hand. The letters which discuss me are numbered, as is the spell which Simone cast upon me, and her *Greetings to Sylvie and the seven devils which dwell inside her since my visit,* a sentence which once truly baffled me, for I looked within myself for these mysterious devils, waiting for them to appear, and do something amazing. Jokes, secrets, teasing, hope, grief, affection, and kisses are all numbered. My family is numbered. But this is no time for emotion, as a female prison guard is hurrying over, telling me, "Watch out! Don't crease them."

I might have spent my entire childhood, teen years, and several decades of adult life not just creasing all the letters, but folding them into little boats, chewing on them, and drooling on them. I did not do so. Why would I do it now?

I know that I cause concern by caressing with my eyes and fingers these pages covered with familiar handwriting, resonant phrases, and the laughs and sighs which marked my childhood. And also because I smile at them. I smile at my grandparents. I lift a page and balance it on my palm. It is so light, so cheerful, so filled with hope and life. My grandmother writes to Simone, who is traveling in Italy: *My dear little sweetheart, Once again, what a delight your letter was. Nothing could please me more than your getting acquainted with this country which was made for you, and the resulting harmony which sings in your letters.*

Later, I too would be her dear little sweetheart.

On another page I can see so clearly my grandfather Biri, whose solid, down-to-earth medical common sense never left him: *But do not let the museums, churches, etc. make you forget that human beings have stomachs which need to be nourished so that the body can fend off fatigue.*

Each of the last two boxes opened contains its own pathetic jumble of faded postcards, copybooks, and notebooks decorated with drawings. A canvas pouch stitched by Mime to keep her daughter's notebooks inside. Simone's change purse. Biri's address book. "How touching," says one of the female jailers, with a smile that strives to be emotional but only manages to seem greedy. She fingers the canvas pouch, wanting me to witness her spurious tender feelings. I shut my ears. I am deaf.

At the bottom of one box is a leather luggage label-holder, which was Simone's. On the tag portion is carefully penned in my grandmother's handwriting: "Miss Simone Weil, Fighting French Highquarters, 4 Carlton Gardens, London SW 1." The word "Highquarters" is an error, cobbling together "Headquarters" and "High Command." I suspect that Selma is confused and deathly sad. But she has always helped Simone, and now she is still helping her to prepare for this departure which breaks her heart. This label-holder gave me a start. It is identical to the ones which I saw year after year attached to André's different suitcases, since he would switch them, opting for progressively lightweight luggage as he grew older. Suddenly I can hear the almost solemn way in which he would say: "A suitcase is packed like a puzzle. Everything must fit together perfectly."

It pleases me to think that it was Biri who, in Marseilles, gave each of them a label-holder. Yes, Bernard, as a good father, wanted, even in these times of war, to give his children something useful. Here, these things come in handy, and they're strong, they will last. The Weils have always liked good-quality, genuine leather, thick-soled shoes which are ugly but hard-wearing.

André's label-holder is now in my desk drawer. It is completely threadbare and shriveled, its leather tarnished.

While Simone barely used hers. It is still brand-new. Just one round trip from France to America and back to England. And now at the bottom of the box.

I obtained weekend parole for my grandfather's address book. Obtained is not the correct word. In truth, I bitterly negotiated this parole, and even left the saint's Gregorian Missal behind as hostage. The day when, some time before my father's death, they came to the rue Auguste-Comte to empty the manuscripts cupboard, as well as an armoire full of books, notebooks, and copybooks, those officiating over this raid had neglected the missal.

Biri's address book is very comfortable at my place, much more so than in the box where it sat rotting for fifteen years. This book used to live next to the telephone, even during my childhood when many of the people listed there were already dead, and had been carefully crossed out. In it I now find the daily life of a doctor, at a time when doctors traveled, with patients' addresses and means of transportation.

There are also a bunch of useful addresses of plumbers, telephone operators, masseurs and masseuses, a physical education teacher. There is a certain Kergoat on the rue de Vaugirard, followed by the comment, "potatoes." Did he pay for medical visits in potatoes?

Some pages are brimming with Haguenauer, Vormus, Weil, and Weill cousins. The "B" page, which the Baumann family should fill, has been torn out. By whom and for what reason? I often wondered how Biri could have earned a living, given the amount of time which he spent attending to the illnesses of his vast family, all of whom he naturally treated for nothing. In a letter to the still-youthful André, Biri teasingly writes: *I worked a bit this past month, but my last winter's fees are not getting paid. We may after all have to sell the books and papers you left here in order to bail ourselves out.* Just a joke? I am not sure.

André and Simone were very proud of their father. When André played in the Luxembourg Gardens, if he heard a playmate cough, or merely sneeze, he would immediately recommend Doctor Weil, reciting the phone number and office hours at the top of his lungs: "Monday, Wednesday, and Friday from 1:30 to 3 P.M.!" During their student days or as adults, Simone and André always sent their friends to see their father, trusting only in him.

I can see my grandfather walking unhurriedly, an Alsatian who likes to take his time, *get off at the Bécon-les-Bruyères stop, turn left after exiting the station*, a modest little man usually in a fine mood, *take the S to the porte Champerret*, carrying sweets or sometimes a book to the young cousins whose measles or mumps he was treating, *Asnières, get off on the engine side*, washing his hands as soon as he arrived, then sitting on the patient's bed. If it was a child, he stared at him with his brown eyes, and began by exhaling loudly: "Hoo!" Then he would stick his ear to the child's stomach and chest, and the small patient would giggle because his moustache was scratchy.

I too can still feel Biri's moustache against my stomach. And I decided to permanently extend the notebook's parole. Bernard certainly deserves to stay for a time with his granddaughter.

Revelation

Around twenty years after my bout of pneumonia and the tunnel episode, my aunt appeared to me again. She seemed to have taken lessons in civility from the Almighty, who always calls twice, out of courtesy, but also love, or *hibah*, as Rashi's biblical commentary explains this repetition. So she called me twice, using the nickname which she gave me before I was born.

"Patapon, Patapon, listen to me."

This time, I perceived immense affection in her somewhat dry voice.

"Listen carefully," she said. "Open your ears, oh my pseudo-niece with the sunny smile. I had cast a spell on you, while you greedily quaffed your baby bottle, and I thought that with time, more gray matter would have developed, but no, you still do not get it. I cannot let you live out the remainder of your life without understanding who you are. So you never guessed? They managed to hide it from you all right, but your name is similar to mine, and look at your face. Did you ever ask yourself why your grandparents felt such a possessive love for you that they wanted to keep you for themselves? Did you not find the dates of my compulsory stay in New York to be suspicious? Do you think that I would have agreed to leave France for any other reason? There was simply no question of bringing a little Weil into the world in German-occupied France. You surely read the letters in which I endlessly begged all of them to tell me about you. Did you not perceive in my wish to have you baptized, which always grieved you, a natural wish to protect you, and ensure your happiness? I wanted everything for you.

"Then there was Eveline. I really thought that she would finally spill the beans. You were so obviously the least loved of her three children, to the point where one day, the housemaid asked: 'What have you got against Sylvie? She always gets good grades in school.' You were ten years old at the time. As you see, I know everything about you. Later, when your classmates saw you two together, they were convinced that she was your stepmother, not your mother.

"Do you recall the tone she adopted when she sometimes said: 'Oh, you just made a gesture which Simone might have made.' It was not a pleased or soft-hearted tone. Instead, it was as if she noticed something irritating.

"I wanted happiness for you, and as you know, marriage. You were amused by what I say in a letter to André: 'I hope to see her again before her wedding.' I wanted you to be happy in the most middle-class way. Consider what models I had around me! In any case, I did not want you to be anything like me.

"Obviously, you wonder who might have been your father? A union organizer, a big-hearted, courageous man. He desired me so much, and one time, just once, I . . . You never guessed? It is beyond belief."

She vanished, and I started to laugh. So the Red Virgin was not so virginal after all? So she found a means of manufacturing me? Where did it happen? And why? Out of simple curiosity? To experience the human condition in depth, just as she once visited a whorehouse? To be nice to a Resistance fighter who had to leave Marseilles the following day, and might die the next week at the hands of the German occupiers? To finally expire in a moment of well-earned sensual pleasure, between two meetings or two cigarettes? Was it an instant of passion? Looking at photos of Simone from her teenage years, I always suspected that her much-vaunted asceticism must not have come easily.

I laughed, overwhelmed with joy. Not over being her daughter, since being André's daughter or Simone's amounted to the same thing, really, but because my true place in the family constellation had finally been revealed to me, with dazzling clarity.

Roots

When my father died, my editor Raphaël Sorin wrote to me: "You have lost your father, but you still have Rashi." He did not know the half of it.

Several years before, I had begun to seriously study Hebrew, to immerse myself in our ancestral Judaism, the same Judaism which Simone doggedly refused to experience. Principally, I became enthralled with Shlomo Yitzhaki, known as Rashi. There is a Jewish saying that Rashi is always present in schoolrooms, and he became my classmate.

On the days when I was not teaching, I went to visit André in Princeton. As soon as I arrived, he would ask:

"How is Rashi doing?"

He took an interest in my improvement in Hebrew. I bought a large-print Haggadah (the book of readings for the Passover seder service) for the visually impaired, to explain the basics of the language to him. I told him about Shlomo Yitzhaki's biblical commentaries, and the novel which I was writing, *Les Vendanges de Rachi* (*Rashi's Vintage*).

169

André and my protagonist were aging simultaneously. To describe the elderly Shlomo of Troyes, I observed my father.

At times his eyes are still merry and affectionate, but nonetheless they have lost their lovely warm brown hue. They no longer focus on people or things with the acuteness which people talking to him found so unnerving. It seems to Tam that his grandfather is imprisoned somewhere behind this grayish, bleary gaze. His hands have changed too. They are cold, dry, and discolored. His fingers look transparent.

Even near the end, when a subject interested him enough, André would recover all his conversational verve. As did my Rashi:

Shlomo's voice is warm and unfaltering . . . He has recaptured his own personal way of gesturing with both hands to accentuate his words.

During the last years of his life, André started to use Yiddish words, sometimes telling me: "Your husband the psychiatrist is really nuts, totally meshuga." Some words would pop up, like the names of holidays, Yom Kippur and Rosh Hashanah, which he pronounced "Rosheshona" with a charming Ashkenazi accent.

I would tease him:

"Where does that come from?"

"From the grandmothers, of course."

André and Simone carefully fostered the quaint family fiction which consisted of persuading themselves, and others, that as children, they were unaware that they were Jewish. Simone supposedly learned that she was Jewish when she was eleven years old. Nonetheless, she had already been traumatized by her grandmother, who refused to eat shrimp. When Simone was eleven, André was fourteen. He was named Abraham, he was circumcised, he sometimes visited with his Weil and Reinherz cousins who were fully aware of being Jews. Grandmother Eugénie read her prayer book (in Hebrew, naturally), while grandmother Hermine enjoyed showing the children a collection of Hebrew poems written by her husband. Selma scattered Yiddish words and expressions in her letters (although at a pinch these might be explained away as German terms). The vast majority of Bernard's patients were Jews, as André often told me, since Jews went to a Jewish doctor, while Christians went to a Christian doctor, according to the custom of the day.

"And you expect me to believe that you and your sister were that stupid? Or that every fact seeped into your clever little brains so beautifully, except for that single one?"

My father smiled in response.

He was entertained by the notion that long after he died, a young professor researching a biography of him in Princeton at the Institute library's archives might soon reach the conclusion that towards the end of his life, André Weil returned to Judaism.

Why would the young biographer reach this conclusion? Since the time when I was a girl, I could forge my father's signature perfectly. In his absence, I could sign my report cards as well as permission letters for me to do this or that. At the Institute library, this allowed me to take out books in bulk by using his name, but without disturbing him. So, my father's biographer would discover that André Weil spent the last years of his life reading not just several Talmud treatises, but also studies on the Talmud, Ginzberg's *Legends of the Jews*, Graetz's *History of the Jews*, as well as books on medieval Judaism.

One evening we spoke about this jokingly, and then André told me quite seriously:

"You are doing what my sister would have done eventually, because she was honest, by and large."

The Mirror's Eyes

I WAS THE ONE WHO CLEARED OUT THE APARTMENT ON THE rue Auguste-Comte, into which the Weil family had moved in 1929. And into which they moved back after the war, broken by Simone's death, only to forever tear each other to pieces in the cruel, bitter mourning which cast a gloom over my childhood. A place which I shall, nevertheless, visit in my dreams until I die.

In truth, the apartment which I was clearing out had already been emptied before. My parents' and grandparents' furniture, and even one of the bathtubs, had gone during the Occupation as Jewish property confiscated by the Germans, doubtless sent to molder in fields by the borderline. All that remained were the living-room mirror and its frame, too large and cumbersome to be disassembled and transported, even by highly efficient Germans.

On the final moving day, while a cavalcade of cartons was taken away, I constantly imagined the arrival of the illustrious Weil quartet. The good doctor, his bright and forceful wife, and their two marvelous, brilliant children André and Simone, my father and aunt, the former at twenty-three having received his diploma years before, the latter at twenty still a student at the École Normale Supérieure.

It was precisely seventy years ago.

I imagined them, who knows why, making a running entrance all four at a time, as if they had stood on the landing outside the heavy wooden door, waiting for the go-ahead. Like actors waiting in the wings for their cue. I imagined all four of them, laughing with pleasure and exclaiming at the splendid view. Simone and André went sliding on the brand-new parquet floor. True, they were a bit old for that. Nonetheless, this is how I imagined them. After sliding a few times to please me, they were free to go back to their studies. In any case, there was no sign yet of tables, chairs, or André's wide and very modern desk, custom-made, which he would describe to me later with amused longing. I could see the brother and sister, handsome and jubilant, with their dark hair, identical eyes, the eyes of conniving twins behind nearly identical, round eyeglasses, with slightly thick lips and wry voices echoing among the empty rooms.

Perhaps for once, Simone did not turn away from the mirror and refuse to see her reflection, as was her wont, and which resulted in her going out wearing a sweater backwards or with an ink-stained face, all of which makes up part of her legend. Maybe on that day, her glance would have skittered onto the vast mirror, and observed her slim figure skimming along the new parquet floor. As a young man, André liked to wear dressy clothes, as can be seen in photos showing his natty suits, neatly buttoned vests, and meticulously combed hair with a part in the middle. He would surely have glanced in the mirror.

The mirror had been set into the wall the day before. It occupied the entire space between the living room's two windows in its heavy frame of pseudo-baroque copper, bedecked with patterns of foliage in the then-popular style, blending in with the geometrical forms on the blue wall-covering fabric.

Everything was done according to my grandmother's ideas. She had conceived, arranged, and foreseen everything, and drawn it all with the architect. The building was not finished, the electricity had not yet been turned on, and the Weils were the first to move into their new roost. They were laughing. They were alive and laughing.

My grandfather rubbed his hands together, like a quiet Alsatian who is pleased with life, and whose only wish is for his family to be happy, too.

That afternoon, standing in the center of an echoing room, as on their moving-in day, I could not shake the idea that any minute the door would open and the four Weils would come in, followed by sweating and panting movers. Six flights to climb, and the elevator still not installed. My grandmother would issue orders: the splendid Bechstein piano here, the Empire desk in the doctor's office, the modern desk on the seventh floor overhead. The sideboard goes here, and against the wall, the neat little secretary desk painted in eighteenth-century style, the pride and joy of my great-grandmother Hermine Solomonovna, who was convinced that this "gem" would one day bring a fortune to her descendants. I had recently learned that the so-called "gem," saved by a housemaid from the clutches of the German occupiers and returned to the rue Auguste-Comte, was almost worthless.

Scarcely was the Bechstein in place when my grandmother would play something, then shout that a piano tuner must be called urgently. My grandfather would point out that the phone had not yet been connected.

And all this time, I, their ungrateful granddaughter, was working against them, clearing out the rooms as soon as my grandmother had arranged them, shipping the "gem" to my sister in America, and finally sanctioning the removal of the vast mirror and its baroque frame. Uprooted from the wall and separated from one another, they were the last to leave the apartment, borne on the shoulders of staffers from Mr. Tambourini's secondhand goods shop.

Pale Petals

THE YEAR I WAS BORN, SIMONE WROTE: *THIS ALMOST INFINITE frailty . . . We can think about it on every joyous occasion. We should not if such thinking would disrupt or lessen the joy. But that is not the way things are. Joy only acquires a more piercing and harrowing gentleness, like the frailty of cherry tree blossoms increases their beauty.*

It is raining in Tokyo, raining petals, pale pink petals. In the narrow, somewhat shabby streets of Tsukiji, the harbor district, it is raining petals. On the gigantic corpses of tuna, it is raining petals. And also on the stylish kimono-clad women who scurry with tiny steps through the posh neighborhoods of the Ginza.

On the jackets of the bustling ants whom I, an illiterate fool with only a dozen words at her command, ask for directions, it is raining pale petals.

The illiterate fool strides along the Tokyo streets, laughing to herself. Laughing to find herself overwhelmed by the immensity of it all. She laughs on the escalators which carry her up towards the sky, she laughs as she surveys, from atop complex networks of elevated sidewalks, the wide avenues lined with glass-fronted

175

buildings, vertical, multicolored, and blinding in the sunlight. She laughs, although she sometimes panics, really panics about being a dwarf, an ant among ants, an illiterate fool of an ant, she laughs, although she has to restrain herself in order not to fall into the arms of an Australian couple with whom she exchanges three actual sentences in a familiar language.

Before her trip, when Japanese friends told her she would see the cherry trees, she replied politely: "Yes, cherry trees, they will be pretty, how delightful."

She had not quite understood. She had not realized that for days at a time, she would walk under a shower of petals, that she would see pink rivers, that by night she would join long, slow processions, dark rivers running parallel to rivers white with petals, and like everyone else, would raise her camera high to capture, to retain a tiny portion of the soft and radiantly pink expanse.

She laughs with pleasure under the showers of petals swirling even in treeless streets.

One night, under a full moon, she laughs in surprise in a dreary gray district when, at the corner of a factory building, she is met by the triumphant paleness of a scrawny cherry tree, under which cap-wearing men and blighted-looking women sit eating, drinking, and singing.

She laughs while gathering armfuls of petals, like pinkish, powdery snow.

She had not foreseen that one day, a frail and nearly transparent petal would land on the sleeve of her black raincoat, while she, motionless, would hold her breath so as not to blow it away, she had not foreseen that suddenly her mother would appear before her, frail, and merry, lying on the ground beneath a flowering cherry tree, saying she would love to be snatched by this glorious pink cloud, to soar, to drown in the cherry tree's rosy softness. Her blue eyes were open wide in wonder, like those of a doll, looking up towards the mound of pale petals. Just a few days later she would be buried, poor dead flower, under a different cherry tree.

No, she had not foreseen that starting from this moment, the moment of the pale petal on her sleeve, she would still laugh but would also be subject to odd seizures, feeling breathless and heavy hearted at unexpected moments, in a souvenir shop, for instance, looking at rows of *kokeshi*, armless and legless dolls with wobbly round heads, which her mother was crazy about, perhaps because of their simplicity and obvious fragility. Or again, foolishly, as a taxi passes by, and she remembers that her father, having returned from a long stay in Japan, always spoke of "taking a *takushi*."

Under the rain of pale petals, she continues to walk, gets lost, finds her way again, apologizes, exclaims "Oh, so sorry!" bows and laughs at the number of bows which mark life on the anthill. She shakes her hair to free the petals which have landed there. Yet she has lost the innocence, self-confidence, and sleek exterior of a tired but serene tourist. From now on, struck and wounded, she feels as frail and wobbly as the *kokeshi*. Frail as her mother carried off by a cloud of petals.

At Yokohama, the wind is blowing. A storm of pale petals beats down on the vast square of one of the world's largest shopping centers, the brand-new Minato Mirai 21. Which does not prevent a tiny girl in a red hat, a child of the twenty-first century, still unsteady on her feet, from chasing after pigeons, beneath one of the tallest Ferris wheels in the world.

Long ago in New York, a little girl ran after pigeons, watched by her refugee grandparents, grieving and humiliated in a world entirely different from their own.

My grandmother wrote: *Today Bernard will go and buy a raincoat for our princess, because it rains a lot.*

Under the tremendous, humming Minato Mirai Ferris wheel, a foolish and illiterate ant on the verge of tears, I suddenly imagine my grandfather drifting through a department store, where no one spoke any language he knew, looking for a raincoat. So that no shower or drizzle might prevent his little princess from chasing after pigeons. During his exile in the New World, did my grandfather ever run into another old Alsatian Jew with whom he might exchange a couple of silly old jokes, cheerfully rubbing his hands together all the while? With whom he could imagine for a moment being on a peaceful street in Wolfisheim?

The little girl with the red hat totters in front of me. I smile at her. She bows to me. I bow to her in return. She laughs and runs away. In a few weeks, far from here, pink petals will rain on my parents' gravestone.

Epilogue

An extremely pleasant man whom I met when he was working on a project involving Simone Weil announced at the end of one of our conversations:

"At least with you, I lucked out."

I smiled expectantly, waiting to hear more, since compliments are always nice. I was expecting a compliment on my attentiveness, sense of humor, reasonable ideas, and personal charm. The compliment appeared in an unexpected guise:

"I might have had to deal with a half-wit."

This was said in the nicest possible way, without irony or pretension. He genuinely seemed to think that he had had a close escape. I admit that for a moment, I was dumbstruck.

"A half-wit?"

"Sure, the last of the line, so to speak. First the grandparents who are extraordinary, if not geniuses, who beget and raise two geniuses, Simone and André. Then the two geniuses. After that, the third generation is not a foregone conclusion."

"In short, André and Simone might have exhausted the stock of gray matter allocated to the Weil family?"

179

"Yes, more or less."

"Statistically speaking, then, I should be a half-wit."

He smiled and nodded his head.

I burst out laughing. Simone, my grandparents, and father, who shared a special vocabulary and some expressions which I find in family letters, as well as in my aunt's writings, would say "I fell about laughing."

I think of this conversation from time to time. I am unimaginably pleased and proud not to be a total half-wit!

Sylvie Weil is the niece of Simone Weil and the daughter of André Weil. She earned her degrees in classics and French literature at the Sorbonne. She has been a professor of French literature at Hunter College and at the Graduate Center of the City University of New York and has also taught at Barnard College and Bennington College. She is the author of several award-winning works of fiction for adults and for young adults. *Le mazal d'Elvina* won the Prix Sorcières for the best novel for young people in France. Two of Sylvie Weil's novels have been published in the United States: *My Guardian Angel* (2004) and *Elvina's Mirror* (2009).

Benjamin Ivry's previous books include biographies of Arthur Rimbaud, Maurice Ravel, and Francis Poulenc. He has translated such authors as André Gide, Jules Verne, Balthus, and Witold Gombrowicz.